中外文稀有版本文献

《法兰西内战》

②

英 文 版

【德】卡尔·马克思 ◎ 著

《法兰西内战》的出版与传播[①]

（代序）

作为出生和成长于比较落后的德国的马克思，对于法国大革命以来的这段历史非常关注。著有《1848至1850年的法兰西阶级斗争》《路易·波拿巴的雾月十八日》等重要著作，充分显示了他的历史唯物主义方法的科学性及其理论的力量和预见性。巴黎公社起因于普法战争，在写作《法兰西内战》之前，马克思还起草了国际工人协会总委员会关于普法战争的两篇宣言。因为这两篇宣言与后来写的《法兰西内战》关系密切，而且，马克思在写《法兰西内战》时也提到了第二篇宣言，所以，恩格斯1891年编辑《法兰西内战》单行本时收入了这两篇宣言。为此，恩格斯写道："在上面提到的这篇篇幅较大的著作前面，我加上了总委员会关于普法战争的两篇较短的宣言。首先，是因为《内战》提到了第二篇宣言，而第二篇宣言如果没有第一篇宣言作参照，是不能完全弄明白的。其次是因为这两篇同为马克思所写的宣言，也和《内战》一样，突出地显示了作者在《路易·波拿巴的雾月十八日》中已经初次表现出的惊人的才能，即在伟大历史事变还在我们眼前展开或者刚刚终结时，就能准确地把握住这些事变的性质、意义及其必然后果。"[②]

[①] 本内容主要参照和引用了《马克思恩格斯文集》第3卷中的题注资料和人民出版社1976年1月编印的《马克思恩格斯著作的发表和出版》一书，原著为前苏联学者列文所著，1948年在苏联出版。

[②] 《马克思恩格斯文集》第3卷，北京：人民出版社2009年版，第99页。

一　《国际工人协会总委员会关于普法战争的第一篇宣言》的写作与早期传播

《国际工人协会总委员会关于普法战争的第一篇宣言》是马克思在1870年7月19—23日写成的。

1870年7月19日，即在拿破仑三世的政府狂妄地向普鲁士宣战的当天，总委员会委托马克思起草关于这次战争的宣言。宣言在7月23日的总委员会常委会上通过，在1870年7月26日的总委员会会议上被一致批准。宣言首先用英文刊登在伦敦1870年7月28日《派尔－麦尔新闻》第1702号上，几天以后以传单的形式印行了1000份。英国的许多地方报纸也全文或摘要转载了宣言。宣言曾送交《泰晤士报》编辑部，但该报拒绝发表。

鉴于宣言的第一版很快就脱销，1870年8月2日总委员会决定再增印1000份。同年9月，第一篇宣言又和总委员会关于普法战争的第二篇宣言一起用英文再版；马克思在这一版中更正了第一篇宣言在第一版中的几个印刷错误。

8月9日，总委员会成立了一个委员会，负责把第一篇宣言翻译成德文和法文并加以传播。参加这个委员会的有：马克思、荣克、赛拉叶和埃卡留斯。宣言由威·李卜克内西翻译成德文首次发表在1870年8月7日莱比锡《人民国家报》第63号上。马克思得到宣言的这个德译文之后，对译文作了彻底的加工，对全文的几乎一半重新进行了翻译。宣言的新的德译文刊登在1870年8月《先驱》杂志第8期上，同时还印成传单，随后，还发表在8月12日纽约《工人联合报》、8月13日苏黎世《哨兵报》第26号、8月13日维也纳《人民意志报》第26号以及8月21日奥格斯堡《无产者报》第56号上。1891年纪念巴黎公社20周年的时候，恩格斯在柏林《前进报》出版社出版的《法兰西内战》德文版上刊出了总委员会关于普法战争的第一篇宣言和第二篇宣言，这两篇宣言的译者是路易莎·考茨基夫人，恩格斯对译文进行了校订。

总委员会关于普法战争的第一篇宣言用法文发表在1870年8月日内瓦《平等报》第28号、1870年8月7日布鲁塞尔《国际报》第82号和1870年8月7日韦尔维耶《米拉波报》第55号上。宣言还由总委员会所设委员会译成法文印成传单。第一篇宣言于1870年8—9月首次用俄文发表在日内瓦出版的《人民事业》第6—7期上。

二 《国际工人协会总委员会关于普法战争的第二篇宣言》的写作与早期传播

《国际工人协会总委员会关于普法战争的第二篇宣言》是马克思在1870年9月6—9日写成的。

1870年9月6日,国际总委员会研究了由于第二帝国崩溃及普法战争进入一个新阶段而形成的新局势,决定就普法战争发表第二篇宣言。为此,成立了一个起草委员会,其成员有马克思、荣克、米尔纳和赛拉叶。

马克思起草这篇宣言时,利用了恩格斯寄给他的各种材料,这些材料揭露了普鲁士军阀、容克(地主)和资产阶级借口军事战略上的需要而并吞法国领土的野心。总委员会在1870年9月9日召开专门会议,一致通过了马克思起草的这一宣言。宣言被分送到伦敦各资产阶级报纸,这些报纸却采取沉默态度,只有《派尔-麦尔新闻》在1870年9月16日摘要刊登了宣言。9月11—13日宣言用英文以传单的形式印行1000份。9月底又出版了将第一篇和第二篇宣言印在一起的新版本。这一版改正了第一版的几个印刷错误,也对个别段落的文字作了修改。

第二篇宣言的德文本是由马克思翻译的,他在翻译时删去了个别段落,增加了几句专门针对德国工人说的话。第二篇宣言的这个译本发表在1870年10—11月《先驱》杂志第10—11期,1870年10月8日维也纳《人民意志报》第37号以及1870年10月1日苏黎世《哨兵报》第

33号上，同时还以传单的形式在日内瓦印行。1891年，恩格斯在《法兰西内战》的德文第三版中刊出了第二篇宣言，为该版翻译第二篇宣言的是路易莎·考茨基夫人，恩格斯对译文进行了校订。

第二篇宣言的法译文载于1870年10月23日《国际报》第93号和12月4日的第99号，1870年9月21日《波尔多论坛报》，并以节译的形式载于1870年10月4日《平等报》第35号。此外，这篇宣言还用弗拉芒文发表于1872年10月16日和24日安特卫普《工人报》第51号和52号。

三 《法兰西内战》的写作与早期传播

马克思和恩格斯始终热情地关心巴黎劳动者的斗争，高度赞扬巴黎工人的英雄气概和革命首创精神。他们在伦敦利用一切可能与巴黎公社取得联系，给予支持和帮助。马克思亲自给了巴黎公社许多宝贵的指示，并且给第一国际各支部发出了数百封信，号召各国工人援助巴黎公社。公社革命期间，国际总委员会先后举行了7次会议，专门讨论公社问题。马克思还与公社委员弗兰克尔、莱奥、瓦尔兰建立了通信联系。公社失败后，第一国际及其各国支部强烈抗议反动派镇压公社，谴责梯也尔政府的暴行，发动营救、支援和救济公社流亡者的活动。在5月28日凌晨巴黎公社最后的147名社员于拉雪兹神甫公墓东北角的墙下全部被反动军队屠杀的第三天，即5月30日，马克思就在第一国际总委员会会议上宣读了他的著名著作《法兰西内战》，全面论述了巴黎公社的丰功伟绩，总结了巴黎公社的经验和教训，揭露和痛斥了梯也尔反动政府官员们的丑恶嘴脸及其镇压公社的罪恶行径。

巴黎公社一宣布成立，马克思就开始细心搜集和研究所有关于公社活动的消息，如当时能够收集到的法国、英国、德国报刊的材料，巴黎来信提供的情况等。最初，马克思曾在1871年3月28日总委员会会议上提出发表一篇告巴黎工人的宣言,这项建议被一致通过,并委托马克思起草这个文件。马克思接受了这个委托,并准备起草这个文件。但是,巴黎的局势发生了变化,一是马克思已经观察到,巴黎这场武装反对鲁普士军队的民族战争正在演化为一场法国反动政府勾结普鲁士军队镇压巴黎公社的国内战争,形势究竟如何发展,还需要作进一步的观察。二是当时法国社会上有一种论调,认为巴黎无产阶级的革命行动是根据国际总委员会的指示进行的,巴黎公社直接领导了这次起义和建立公社的行动。在这样的情况下发表告巴黎工人书,可能时机不合适。

　　经过一段时间的观察与研究,马克思逐渐对巴黎公社的性质和巴黎工人阶级革命的历史意义有了清楚的认识。马克思在4月12日给库格曼的信中充分肯定了巴黎工人阶级打碎资产阶级国家机器的伟大创举。马克思这时一反过去曾经认为巴黎的行为是一件蠢事的说法,指出:巴黎工人的行动如果有什么不足的话,那就是对于敌人过于宽容,没有像第一巴黎公社时期一样及时地向凡尔赛进军,因为他们不愿发动国内战争。这两个错误是中央委员会过早地放弃了领导权,过早地把权力移交给了公社。4月17日,马克思再次给库格曼写信指出:"工人阶级反对资本家阶级及其国家的斗争由于巴黎人的斗争而进入了一个新阶段。不管这件事情的直接结果怎样,具有世界历史意义的新起点毕竟是已经取得了。"这就是说,在巴黎公社正式成立的两周之后,马克思就已经准确地预见到了这场斗争的结局。所以他充分地肯定了巴黎人民的这次伟大的悲壮之举,特别是肯定了巴黎工人阶级打碎资产阶级国家机器的伟大尝试,认为单凭这一点,他们就将永载史册。在马克思看来,巴黎人民这种打碎资产阶级国家机器的举动是所有欧洲大陆国家工人阶级取得革命胜利的先决条件。

　　马克思这时候意识到,现在不是要发表一篇告巴黎工人的宣言,告诉巴黎工人如何行动和指导整个运动的进展,而是要向全世界工人阶级发出呼吁,呼吁全世界的工人阶级一起行动起来,同情和支持巴黎工阶级的伟大壮举。于是马克思在1871年4月18日总委员会会议上，建议就法国"斗争的总趋向"发表一篇告国际全体会员的宣言。马克思的建议得到一致通过，总委员会继续委托马克思起草这一宣言。会后，马克思就开始了宣言的起草工作。

这里所谓宣言，指的就是马克思后来写成的《法兰西内战——国际工人协会总委员会宣言》。马克思写这个宣言用了两个多月的时间。如果从3月18日巴黎起义他开始建立笔记和摘录到5月30日马克思在国际大会上宣读这个宣言为止，他用去了70多天的时间。在这期间，他除了处理国际工人协会的日常事务之外，还要参加总委员会的各种会议，要同各地工人运动的领导人和其他友人进行联络，帮助他们开展工作。巴黎公社成立之后，马克思的工作更加忙碌，他同公社一些负责人保持联系，同来往于巴黎和伦敦之间的有关人员谈话，对公社的工作提意见和建议；他要组织撰写文章和稿件，对有关报刊和反对者对巴黎革命和国际工人协会的造谣、中伤和污蔑进行回击和反驳；他要组织各国工人集会声援巴黎公社。马克思在这期间写了几百封关于巴黎公社的信，寄给所有建立了国际组织的国家，通过这些信件，阐明巴黎公社的无产阶级性质和重大历史意义，呼吁他们给巴黎公社以积极的支持和帮助。所以说，《法兰西内战》几乎是在百忙之中抽空写出来的。恩格斯在5月9日的总委员会会议上向大家报告说："公民马克思病得很重，宣言的起草工作使他的病更加恶化了。"这主要是他的支气管炎发作引起咳嗽，妨碍睡眠，同时他的慢性肝病也因为长时间休息不好而严重起来。从4月中旬到6月中旬，马克思断断续续病了两个月。他就是在这样的情况下完成了《法兰西内战》的写作。

从巴黎革命的第一天起，马克思就着手收集各种报刊，进行摘录，写在笔记本上。由于巴黎处于被封锁状态，得到巴黎的报刊比较困难，马克思主要是利用英国出版的英文和法文报刊如自由派报纸《每日新闻》《回声报》《观察报》，保守派报纸《每日电讯》《旗帜报》，以及半官方的《泰晤士报》、爱尔兰民族主义者办的《爱尔兰人报》和一个波拿巴主义报纸《形势报》。马克思还设法从法国弄到一些巴黎出版的法文报刊，如支持公社的《口令报》《号召报》《波尔多论坛报》《复仇者报》《先锋报》，以及资产阶级报纸《自由报》《费加罗报》《钟报》《小报》等。其他摘录的报纸还有《自由巴黎报》《人民呼声报》《公社报》《人民报》《社会报》《国民报》《形势报》《观察家报》等。马克思主要是通过这些报纸了解情况，掌握事件的进程和方向。马克思摘录这些报刊资料的笔记已经收入了《马克思恩格斯文库》俄文版第3卷。北京商务印书馆1975年编译出版了由吴惕安等译、陈叔平编的《马克思关于巴黎公社报刊消息摘录》一书。本书附录收入了其中的第一部分。

除了这些报刊资料以外，马克思还利用了巴黎的国际会员和其他友人来信中的资料，如列·弗兰克尔、路·欧·瓦尔兰、奥·赛拉叶、伊·鲁·托马诺夫斯卡娅、彼·拉甫洛夫、保尔·拉法格以及公社其他领导成员的信件和通过他们转交的信件中提供的资料①。

4月18日后，马克思开始这项文献的起草工作，一直继续到5月底。他根据每天整理的材料，先写了《法兰西内战》的初稿和二稿。根据吴惕安研究员考证，"初稿大约是从1871年4月18日写起，到5月9日和13日之间完成。之后就写二稿，二稿大约于5月23日写成。最后的定稿是在5月30日之前写完的"②。1871年5月30日，即巴黎最后一个街垒陷落的两天以后，总委员会一致批准了马克思宣读的《法兰西内战》的定稿文本。随后，马克思又对这一宣言的第四部分的某些段落作了补充和加工。

---

① 这里和以下的部分内容作者参阅和吸收了中央编译局已故同事吴惕安研究员的研究成果《马克思〈法兰西内战〉一书的写作与传播》，见《马列著作编译资料》第9辑。吴惕安研究员在文中提了更多更翔实的资料，可供进一步的研究者查阅。

② 中央编译局：《马列著作编译资料》第9辑，北京：人民出版社1981年版，第139页。

《法兰西内战》最初于1871年6月13日左右在伦敦用英文印成35页的小册子发表，印数1000份，当时没有署作者名字。小册子出版后产生了爆炸性的影响，引起了人们的广泛关注。只用了两天时间第一次印刷的书就销售一空。伦敦几家最大的报纸（《泰晤士报》等）都为这部著作发表社论，英国几乎所有的报纸都相继发表了评论，之后其他各国的报纸也都开始发表有关这部著作的评论文章。正如恩格斯所说："伦敦有史以来还没有一个出版物像国际总委员会宣言那样产生如此强烈的影响。"①

　　在巴黎公社受到资产阶级舆论疯狂攻击的情况下，马克思的《法兰西内战》成了当时唯一指出巴黎公社世界历史意义的著作。资产阶级舆论在攻击巴黎公社和《法兰西内战》的同时，也把攻击的矛头对准了马克思。马克思曾经写道："我目前荣幸地成了伦敦受诽谤最多的、受威胁最大的人。"②恩格斯则通报说："整个伦敦都只是谈论我们。当然是一片狂叫。这样更好。"③马克思为伦敦的这种"极大的惊恐"而感到高兴。他写道："在度过了二十年单调的沼泽地的田园生活之后，这的确是很不错的。"④英国政府办的报纸《观察家报》威胁《法兰西内战》的作者，说要向法庭控告他侮辱镇压巴黎公社的梯也尔政府官员。为了不使总委员会受到打击，马克思在给伦敦一家报纸编辑部的信中宣称他是《法兰西内战》的作者，他愿意个人承担评论梯也尔、法夫尔等人的责任。他写道："对这帮恶棍我一点也不在乎！"⑤——他这样骄傲地回答了要向法庭控告他的威胁。⑥

　　1871年6月27日马克思向总委员会报告说，第一版已销售一空，

---

① 见《马克思恩格斯著作的发表和出版》（内部资料），北京：人民出版社1976年版，第51页。
② 《马克思恩格斯全集》第33卷，北京：人民出版社1956年版，第236页。
③ 《马克思恩格斯全集》第33卷，北京：人民出版社1956年版，第238页。
④ 《马克思恩格斯全集》第33卷，北京：人民出版社1956年版，第236页。
⑤ 《马克思恩格斯全集》第33卷，北京：人民出版社1956年版，第237页。
⑥ 以上文字参考和引用了〔苏〕列·阿·列文凯瑟：《马克思恩格斯著作的发表和出版》，周维译，北京：生活·读书·新知三联书店1976年版一书。

并建议再印2000份。总委员会同意了马克思的建议，不久便出了英文第二版，印数2000份。与此同时《法兰西内战》还由爱·特鲁拉夫于1871年7月1日以传单的形式发行。马克思和恩格斯一起在第二版中改动了几处正文，更正了第一版的几个印刷错误，并增补了《附录》的第二部分。宣言的署名作了如下变动：去掉工联主义者本·鲁克拉夫特和乔·奥哲尔的名字（他们在资产阶级报刊上表示不同意宣言，并退出了总委员会），增添了总委员会新成员的名字。1871年7月25日马克思向总委员会通报说，第二版又已脱销。总委员会根据恩格斯的提议，于1871年8月初出了《法兰西内战》英文第三版，印数1000份，马克思在这一版中删去了前两版中个别不确切的地方。

1871—1872年，《法兰西内战》被译成法文、德文、俄文、意大利文、西班牙文、荷兰文、弗拉芒文、塞尔维亚-克罗地亚文、丹麦文以及波兰文，在欧洲各国和美国的期刊上发表，同时还出了单行本。

德译文是由恩格斯翻译的，1871年6—7月发表于《人民国家报》（6月28日，7月1、5、8、12、16、19、22、26和29日第52—61号），1871年8—10月在《先驱》杂志上摘要发表，此外，还在莱比锡出版了单行本。恩格斯在翻译时作了几处不大的改动。1876年，为了纪念巴黎公社5周年，出版了《法兰西内战》的新德文本，对文字作了一些订正。

《法兰西内战》的法译文于1871年7月6日至9月3日在布鲁塞尔的《国际报》上刊出，同年8月3日至10月21日在日内瓦的《平等报》上刊出。1872年在布鲁塞尔根据英文第三版翻译出版了法文版单行本，译文经马克思校订过，他曾作了大量修改，把某些段落重新译过。布鲁塞尔的法文版一共印了9000册。

1891年，为迎接巴黎公社20周年而准备出《法兰西内战》的德文第三版（纪念版）时，恩格斯重新校订了译文，并为该版写了导言。恩格斯把马克思写的国际工人协会总委员会关于普法战争的第一篇和第二篇宣言收进了这一版。此后在各种文字的单行本中，导言和两篇宣言也都与《法兰西内战》一起刊印。柏林《前进报》出版了这个纪念版。恩格斯在导言中对巴黎公社的历史意义和巴黎公社的经验再次进行了论述。恩格斯在这个单行本中同时也对巴黎公社的历史,其中包括参加公社的布朗基派和蒲鲁东派的活动,作了一系列补充。

四　马克思《法兰西内战》在中国的传播

陈独秀在《新青年》1922年7月第9卷第6号上发表了《马克思学说》一文,在文章中对马克思的《法兰西内战》的部分内容进行了引译,同时引译的还有《共产党宣言》《哥达纲领批判》等。[①]《法兰西内战》第一个中文版本是在抗日战争时期由时任中宣部副部长的吴黎平和刘云（张闻天,又名洛甫）合译,延安解放社1938年11月出版。当时是在物质条件极为困难的情况下,以"马克思恩格斯丛书"第五种的形式出版。该书共收入了6篇文章,其中包括恩格斯1891年写的"引言",马克思写的两篇国际工人协会总委员会关于普法战争的宣言和一篇国际工人协会总委员会关于法兰西内战的宣言,同时还收进了马克思1871年4月致库格曼论巴黎公社的两封信和列宁在《马克思致库格曼书信集》俄译本中论巴黎公社的文章。同年11月,该版本又由中国出版社作为"马克思恩格斯丛书"重印。重印时改为横排版式并将注释改为脚注,由新知书店发行。1939年2月,重庆新华日报馆又把解放社的版本重印,在大后方广泛发行。同年3月,中国出版社再次重印了吴黎平和刘云译的这个版本。4月15日,上海海潮社出版了由郭和翻译的另一个版本。海潮社于1940年11月又把这本书重新出版,书名改为《巴黎公社》。[②]

[①] 见中央编译局马恩室:《马克思恩格斯著作在中国的传播》,北京:人民出版社1983年版,第263页。

[②] 见中央编译局马恩室:《马克思恩格斯著作在中国的传播》,北京:人民出版社1983年版,第315页。

解放战争时期,《法兰西内战》在解放区和国统区都有流传。1946年5月,生活书店把该书作为"世界学术译丛"之一出版,同时在国统区的上海和重庆两地发行。在解放区,解放社重新出版了10年前的版本,1948年交由华北新华书店发行。1949年1月,中原新华书店也出版了这个版本。3月,东北生活书店把该书作为"马列文库之九"出版,由新中国书局(光华书店)发行。5月,华东新华书店出版印刷该书10000册。

人民出版社重新成立后,1954年11月根据1848年8月解放社的版本重印,出版了小32开本,印数3001册,在全国各地发行。1958年3月又重印了一次,印数增加到7500册。

1961年5月,中共中央编译局为了纪念巴黎公社90周年编译出版了《马克思恩格斯列宁斯大林论巴黎公社》,其中所收的《法兰西内战》有4篇文章是在莫斯科外国文书籍出版局出版的《马克思恩格斯文选》(两卷集)第1卷译文的基础上根据新出版的《马克思恩格斯全集》俄文二版第17卷,参照英文本和德文本加以修改,并在校改过程中个别地方参考了吴黎平、刘云的译文。书中还收进了由张芝联、张广达根据《马克思恩格斯文库》1934年第3卷的英文版译出的马克思写作《法兰西内战》一文时的两个草稿,即初稿和二稿。由新华书店向全国发行。人民出版社于1961年5月同时还根据《马克思恩格斯列宁斯大林论巴黎公社》中的译文,排印出版了《法兰西内战》大32开横排的单行本,是为北京初版。当年印行了5000册,1962年再次加印了10080册。

1963年11月,中共中央编译局根据俄文版编译的《马克思恩格斯全集》第17卷出版中收进了马克思写的关于普法战争的两个宣言和《法兰西内战》一文及其两个草稿。其中关于普法战争的两篇宣言和《法兰西内战》一文是在《马克思恩格斯文选》(两卷集)中文版的基础上,根据英文原文校订的;《法兰西内战》初稿、二稿也根据英文原文作了校订。1964年5月,人民出版社在《法兰西内战》单行本第4

次印刷时又作了改版，除了恩格斯的导言在1961年版的译文的基础上根据《马克思恩格斯全集》俄文第二版第22卷作了一次校订外，其他几篇的译文均按照《马克思恩格斯全集》中文版第17卷中的译文排印。中共中央编译局的这个版本在《法兰西内战》初稿和二稿前增加了"'法兰西内战'草稿"作为其初稿和二稿的篇名，书中附注释169条。同年6月，人民出版社又根据这个版本出版了此书的16开大字本（共4册）。

1970年底，《法兰西内战》第二版第5次印刷时中央编译局又进行了修改，其中恩格斯的序言采用《马克思恩格斯全集》中文版第22卷（1965年5月出版发行）的译文。两篇关于普法战争的宣言、《法兰西内战》一文及其两个草稿都根据《马克思恩格斯文选》和《马克思恩格斯文库》的英文版编译。① 该年6月已经再版了该书的16开大字本。

1972年5月，中共中央编译局采用《马克思恩格斯全集》的译文编辑并由人民出版社出版的《马克思恩格斯选集》第2卷除对《法兰西内战》的初稿和二稿进行了摘录以外，其他各篇（包括恩格斯写的1891年单行本导言）都是全文收录，个别译文经过了重新修订。

1995年6月，中共中央编译局修订出版的《马克思恩格斯选集》第二版把马克思的《法兰西内战》编入了第3卷，篇幅与第一版一样，译文上作了个别修订。

2009年中央编译局编辑出版《马克思恩格斯文集》（10卷本），马克思的《法兰西内战》被编入第3卷，篇幅依然保持《马克思恩格斯选集》的内容，译文则依据有关文本作了变动。恩格斯写的1891年版导言根据《马克思恩格斯全集》德文版第22卷翻译；关于普法战争的两篇宣言则是根据《马克思恩格斯全集》英文版第22卷并参考《马克思恩格斯全集》德文版第17卷翻译；《法兰西内战》正文及其两个草

---

① 以上文字参照周文熙：《法兰西内战的写作及在中国的翻译和出版》，载《教学与研究》1981年第2期。

稿（摘录）则是根据《马克思恩格斯全集》历史考证版第 1 部分第 22 卷并参考《马克思恩格斯全集》德文版第 17 卷翻译。

2012 年 9 月出版的《马克思恩格斯选集》第三版仍然将《法兰西内战》收入了第 3 卷，内容依据《马克思恩格斯文集》作了修改，这是《法兰西内战》最新的版本。

（本文来自 2013 年中央编译出版社出版的李惠斌所著《马克思〈法兰西内战〉研究读本》有关内容。）

Workers of All Countries, Unite!

MARX

The Civil War in France

Progress Publishers
Moscow

Translated from the German

First printing 1948
Reprinted 1952, 1961, 1968, 1972, 1974,
1977, 1979

Printed in the Union of Soviet Socialist Republics

М $\frac{10101-579}{014(01)-79}$ без объявл. 0101010000

CONTENTS

	Page
Introduction. By Frederick Engels	7
FIRST ADDRESS OF THE GENERAL COUNCIL OF THE INTERNATIONAL WORKING MEN'S ASSOCIATION ON THE FRANCO-PRUSSIAN WAR	21
SECOND ADDRESS OF THE GENERAL COUNCIL OF THE INTERNATIONAL WORKING MEN'S ASSOCIATION ON THE FRANCO-PRUSSIAN WAR	26
ADDRESS OF THE GENERAL COUNCIL OF THE INTERNATIONAL WORKING MEN'S ASSOCIATION ON THE CIVIL WAR IN FRANCE, 1871	
I	32
II	44
III	52
IV	68
APPENDIXES	81
Notes	85
NAME INDEX	89

INTRODUCTION
BY FREDERICK ENGELS

I did not anticipate that I would be asked to prepare a new edition of the Address of the General Council of the International on *The Civil War in France*, and to write an introduction to it. Therefore I can only touch briefly here on the most important points.

I am prefacing the longer work mentioned above by the two shorter Addresses of the General Council on the Franco-Prussian War. In the first place, because the second of these, which itself cannot be fully understood without the first, is referred to in *The Civil War*. But also because these two Addresses, likewise drafted by Marx, are, no less than *The Civil War*, outstanding examples of the author's remarkable gift, first proved in *The Eighteenth Brumaire of Louis Bonaparte*, for grasping clearly the character, the import and the necessary consequences of great historical events, at a time when these events are still in progress before our eyes or have only just taken place. And, finally, because today we in Germany are still having to endure the consequences which Marx predicted would follow from these events.

Has that which was declared in the first Address not come to pass: that if Germany's defensive war against Louis Bonaparte degenerated into a war of conquest against the French people, all the misfortunes which befell Germany after the so-called wars of liberation* would

---
* The wars against Napoleon I in 1813-15.—*Ed.*

revive again with renewed intensity? Have we not had a further twenty years of Bismarck's rule, the Exceptional Law¹ and Socialist-baiting taking the place of the prosecutions of demagogues, with the same arbitrary action of the police and with literally the same staggering interpretations of the law?

And has not the prediction been proved to the letter, that the annexation of Alsace-Lorraine would "force France into the arms of Russia," and that after this annexation Germany must either become the avowed servant of Russia, or must, after some short respite, arm for a new war, and, moreover, "a race war against the combined Slavonic and Roman races"? Has not the annexation of the French provinces driven France into the arms of Russia? Has not Bismarck for fully twenty years vainly wooed the favour of the tsar, wooed it with services even more lowly than those which little Prussia, before it became the "first Power in Europe," was wont to lay at Holy Russia's feet? And is there not every day still hanging over our heads the Damocles' sword of war, on the first day of which all the chartered covenants of princes will be scattered like chaff; a war of which nothing is certain but the absolute uncertainty of its outcome; a race war which will subject the whole of Europe to devastation by fifteen or twenty million armed men,–and which is not raging already only because even the strongest of the great military states shrinks before the absolute incalculability of its final result?

All the more is it our duty to make again accessible to the German workers these brilliant proofs, now half-forgotten, of the far-sightedness of international working-class policy in 1870.

What is true of these two Addresses is also true of *The Civil War in France*. On May 28, the last fighters of the Commune succumbed to superior forces on the slopes of Belleville; and only two days later, on May 30, Marx read to the General Council the work in which the historical significance of the Paris Commune is delineated in short, powerful strokes, but with such trenchancy, and above all such truth as has never again been attained in all the mass of literature on this subject.

Thanks to the economic and political development of France since 1789, Paris has been placed for the last fifty years in such a position that no revolution could break out there without assuming a proletarian character, that is to say, without the proletariat, which had bought victory with its blood, advancing its own demands after victory. These demands were more or less unclear and even confused, corresponding to the state of development reached by the workers of Paris at the particular period, but in the last resort they all amounted to the abolition of the class antagonism between capitalists and workers. It is true that no one knew how this was to be brought about. But the demand itself, however indefinitely it still was couched, contained a threat to the existing order of society; the workers who put it forward were still armed; therefore, the disarming of the workers was the first commandment for the bourgeois, who were at the helm of the state. Hence, after every revolution won by the workers, a new struggle, ending with the defeat of the workers.

This happened for the first time in 1848. The liberal bourgeois of the parliamentary opposition held banquets for securing a reform of the franchise, which was to ensure supremacy for their party. Forced more and more, in their struggle with the government, to appeal to the people, they had gradually to yield precedence to the radical and republican strata of the bourgeoisie and petty bourgeoisie. But behind these stood the revolutionary workers, and since 1830 these had acquired far more political independence than the bourgeois, and even the republicans, suspected. At the moment of the crisis between the government and the opposition, the workers began street-fighting; Louis Philippe vanished, and with him the franchise reform; and in its place arose the republic, and indeed one which the victorious workers themselves designated as a "social" republic. No one, however, was clear as to what this social republic was to imply; not even the workers themselves. But they now had arms and were a power in the state. Therefore, as soon as the bourgeois republicans in control felt something like firm ground under their feet, their first aim was to disarm the workers. This took place by driving them into the insurrection of June 1848 by direct breach of faith, by open defiance and the attempt to banish the unemployed to a distant province. The government had taken care to have an overwhelming superiority of force.

After five days' heroic struggle, the workers were defeated. And then followed a blood-bath among the defenceless prisoners, the like of which has not been seen since the days of the civil wars which ushered in the downfall of the Roman republic. It was the first time that the bourgeoisie showed to what insane cruelties of revenge it will be goaded the moment the proletariat dares to take its stand against the bourgeoisie as a separate class, with its own interests and demands. And yet 1848 was only child's play compared with the frenzy of the bourgeoisie in 1871.

Punishment followed hard at heel. If the proletariat was not yet able to rule France, the bourgeoisie could no longer do so. At least not at that period, when the greater part of it was still monarchically inclined, and it was divided into three dynastic parties and a fourth, republican party. Its internal dissensions allowed the adventurer Louis Bonaparte to take possession of all the commanding points —army, police, administrative machinery—and, on December 2, 1851, to explode the last stronghold of the bourgeoisie, the National Assembly. The Second Empire began— the exploitation of France by a gang of political and financial adventurers, but at the same time also an industrial development such as had never been possible under the narrow-minded and timorous system of Louis Philippe, with the exclusive domination of only a small section of the big bourgeoisie. Louis Bonaparte took the political power from the capitalists under the pretext of protecting them, the bourgeois, from the workers, and on the other hand the workers from them; but in return his rule encouraged speculation and industrial activity—in a word, the upsurgence and enrichment of the whole bourgeoisie to an extent hitherto unknown. To an even greater extent, it is true, corruption and mass thievery developed, clustering around the imperial court, and drawing their heavy percentages from this enrichment.

But the Second Empire was the appeal to French chauvinism, was the demand for the restoration of the frontiers of the First Empire, which had been lost in 1814, or at least those of the First Republic. A French empire within the frontiers of the old monarchy and, in fact, within the even more amputated frontiers of 1815—such a thing was impossible for any length of time. Hence the necessity for occasional wars and extensions of frontiers. But no extension of frontiers was so dazzling to the imagination of the French chauvinists as the extension to the German left bank of the Rhine. One square mile on the Rhine was more to them than ten in the Alps or anywhere else. Given the Second Empire, the demand for the restoration of the left bank of the Rhine, either all at once or piecemeal, was merely a question of time. The time came with the Austro-Prussian War of 1866; cheated of the anticipated "territorial compensation" by Bismarck and by his own over-cunning, hesitant policy, there was now nothing left for Napoleon but war, which broke out in 1870 and drove him first to Sedan, and thence to Wilhelmshöhe. [2]

The necessary consequence was the Paris Revolution of September 4, 1870. The Empire collapsed like a house of cards, and the republic was again proclaimed. But the enemy was standing at the gates; the armies of the Empire were either hopelessly encircled at Metz or held captive in Germany. In this emergency the people allowed the Paris deputies to the former legislative body to constitute themselves into a "Government of National Defence." This was the more readily conceded, since, for the purposes of defence, all Parisians capable of bearing arms had enrolled in the National Guard and were armed, so that now the workers constituted a great majority. But very soon the antagonism between the almost completely bourgeois government and the armed proletariat broke into open conflict. On October 31, workers' battalions stormed the Town Hall and captured part of the membership of the government. Treachery, the government's direct breach of its undertakings, and the intervention of some petty-bourgeois battalions set them free again, and in order not to occasion the outbreak of civil war inside a city besieged by a foreign military power, the former government was left in office.

At last, on January 28, 1871, starved Paris capitulated. But with honours unprecedented in the history of war. The forts were surrendered, the city wall stripped of guns, the weapons of the regiments of the line and of the Mobile Guard were handed over, and they themselves considered prisoners of war. But the National Guard kept its weapons and guns, and only entered into an armistice with the victors. And these did not dare enter Paris in triumph. They only dared to occupy a tiny corner of Paris, which, into the bargain, consisted partly of public parks, and even this they only occupied for a few days! And during this time they, who had maintained their encirclement of Paris for 131 days, were themselves encircled by the armed workers of Paris, who kept a sharp watch that no "Prussian" should overstep the narrow bounds of the corner ceded to the foreign conqueror. Such was the respect which the Paris workers inspired in the army before which all the armies of the Empire had laid down their arms; and the Prussian *junkers,* who had come to take revenge at the home of the revolution, were compelled to stand by respectfully, and salute precisely this armed revolution!

During the war the Paris workers had confined themselves to demanding the vigorous prosecution of the fight. But now, when peace had come after the capitulation of Paris, now Thiers, the new supreme head of the government, was compelled to realize that the rule of the propertied classes—big landowners and capitalists—was in constant danger so long as the workers of Paris had arms in their hands. His first action was an attempt to disarm them. On March 18, he sent troops of the line with orders to rob the National Guard of the artillery belonging to it, which had been constructed during the siege of Paris and had been paid for by public subscription. The attempt failed; Paris mobilized as one man for resistance, and war between Paris and the French Government sitting at Versailles was declared. On March 26 the Paris Commune was elected and on March 28 it was proclaimed. The Central Committee of the National Guard, which up to then had carried on the government, handed in its resignation to the Commune after it had first decreed the abolition of the scandalous Paris "Morality Police." On March 30 the Commune abolished conscription and the standing army, and declared the sole armed force to be the National Guard, in which all citizens capable of bearing arms were to be enrolled. It remitted all payments of rent for dwelling houses from October 1870 until April 1871, the amounts already paid to be booked as future rent payments, and stopped all sales of articles pledged in the municipal loan office. On the same day the foreigners elected to the Commune were confirmed in office, because "the flag of the Commune is the flag of the World Republic." On April 1 it was decided that the highest salary to be received by any employee of the Commune, and therefore also by its members themselves, was not to exceed 6,000 francs (4,800 marks). On the following day the Commune decreed the separation of the church from the state, and the abolition of all state payments for religious purposes as well as the transformation of all church property into national property; as a result of which, on April 8, the exclusion from the schools of all religious symbols, pictures, dogmas, prayers—in a word, "of all that belongs to the sphere of the individual's conscience"—was ordered and gradually put into effect. On the 5th, in reply to the shooting, day after day, of captured Commune fighters by the Versailles troops, a decree was issued for the imprisonment of hostages, but it was never carried into execution. On the 6th, the guillotine was brought out by the 137th battalion of the National Guard, and publicly burnt, amid great popular rejoicing. On the 12th the Commune decided that the Victory Column on the *Place Vendôme*, which had been cast from captured guns by Napoleon after the war of 1809, should be demolished as a symbol of chauvinism and incitement to national hatred. This was carried out on May 16. On April 16 it ordered a statistical tabulation of factories which had been closed down by the manufacturers, and the working out of plans for the operation of these factories by the workers formerly employed in them, who were to be organized in co-operative societies, and also plans for the organization of these co-operatives in one great union. On the 20th it abolished night work for bakers, and also the employment offices, which since the Second Empire had been run as a monopoly by creatures appointed by the police—labour exploiters of the first rank; these offices were transferred to the mayoralties of the twenty *arrondissements* of Paris. On April 30 it ordered the closing of the pawnshops, on the ground that they were a private exploitation of the workers, and were in contradiction with the right of the workers to their instruments of labour and to credit. On May 5 it ordered the razing of the Chapel of Atonement, which had been built in expiation of the execution of Louis XVI.

Thus from March 18 onwards the class character of the Paris movement, which had previously been pushed into the background by the fight against the foreign invaders, emerged sharply and clearly. As almost only workers, or recognized representatives of the workers, sat in the Commune, its decisions bore a decidedly proletarian character. Either these decisions decreed reforms which the republican bourgeoisie had failed to pass solely out of cowardice, but which provided a necessary basis for the free activity of the working class—such as the realization of the principle that *in relation to the state*, religion is a purely private matter—or the Commune promulgated decrees which were in the direct interest of the working class and in part cut deeply into the old order of society. In a beleaguered city, however, it was possible to make at most a start in the realization of all this. And from the beginning of May onwards all their energies were taken up by the fight against the armies assembled by the Versailles government in ever-growing numbers.

On April 7 the Versailles troops had captured the Seine crossing at Neuilly, on the western front of Paris; on the other hand, in an attack on the southern front on the 11th they were repulsed with heavy losses by General Eudes. Paris was continually bombarded and, moreover, by the very people who had stigmatized as a sacrilege the bombardment of the same city by the Prussians. These same people now begged the Prussian government for the hasty return of the French soldiers taken prisoner at Sedan and Metz, in order that they might recapture Paris for them. From the beginning of May the gradual arrival of these troops gave the Versailles forces a decided superiority. This already became evident when, on April 23, Thiers broke off the negotiations for the exchange, proposed by the Commune, of the Archbishop of Paris and a whole number of other priests held as hostages in Paris, for only one man, Blanqui, who had twice been elected to the Commune but was a prisoner in Clairvaux. And even more from the changed language of Thiers; previously procrastinating and equivocal, he now suddenly became insolent, threatening, brutal. The Versailles forces took the redoubt of Moulin Saquet on the southern front, on May 3; on the 9th, Fort Issy, which had been completely reduced to ruins by gunfire; on the 14th, Fort Vanves. On the western front they advanced gradually, capturing the numerous villages and buildings which extended up to the city wall, until they reached the main defences; on the 21st, thanks to treachery and the carelessness of the National Guards stationed there, they succeeded in forcing their way into the city. The Prussians, who held the northern and eastern forts, allowed the Versailles troops to advance across the land north of the city, which was forbidden ground to them under the armistice, and thus to march forward, attacking on a wide front, which the Parisians naturally thought covered by the armistice, and therefore held only weakly. As a result of this, only a weak resistance was put up in the western half of Paris, in the luxury city proper; it grew stronger and more tenacious the nearer the incoming troops approached the eastern half, the working-class city proper. It was only after eight days' fighting that the last defenders of the Commune succumbed on the heights of Belleville and Menilmontant; and then the massacre of defenceless men, women and children, which had been raging all through the week on an increasing scale, reached its zenith. The breechloaders could no longer kill fast enough; the vanquished were shot down in hundreds by *mitrailleuse* fire. The "Wall of the Federals"* at the Père Lachaise cemetery, where the final mass murder was consummated, is still standing today, a mute but eloquent testimony to the frenzy of which the ruling class is capable as soon as the working class dares to stand up for its rights. Then, when the slaughter of them all proved to be impossible, came the mass arrests, the shooting of victims arbitrarily selected from the prisoners' ranks, and the removal of the rest to great camps where they awaited trial by courts-martial. The Prussian troops surrounding the northeastern half of Paris had orders not to allow any fugitives to pass; but the officers often shut their eyes when the soldiers paid more obedience to the dictates of humanity than to those of the Supreme Command; particular honour is due to the Saxon army corps, which behaved very humanely and let through many who were obviously fighters for the Commune.

---

* Now usually called The Wall of the Communards.—*Ed.*

* * *

If today, after twenty years, we look back at the activity and historical significance of the Paris Commune of 1871, we shall find it necessary to make a few additions to the account given in *The Civil War in France*.

The members of the Commune were divided into a majority, the Blanquists, who had also been predominant in the Central Committee of the National Guard; and a minority, members of the International Working Men's Association, chiefly consisting of adherents of the Proudhon school of Socialism. The great majority of the Blanquists were at that time Socialists only by revolutionary, proletarian instinct; only a few had attained greater clarity on principles, through Vaillant, who was familiar with German scientific Socialism. It is therefore comprehensible that in the economic sphere much was left undone which, according to our view today, the Commune ought to have done. The hardest thing to understand is certainly the holy awe with which they remained standing respectfully outside the gates of the Bank of France. This was also a serious political mistake. The bank in the hands of the Commune—this would have been worth more than ten thousand hostages. It would have meant the pressure of the whole of the French bourgeoisie on the Versailles government in favour of peace with the Commune. But what is still more wonderful is the correctness of much that nevertheless was done by the Commune, composed as it was of Blanquists and Proudhonists. Naturally, the Proudhonists were chiefly responsible for the economic decrees of the Commune, both for their praiseworthy and their unpraiseworthy aspects; as the Blanquists were for its political commissions and omissions. And in both cases the irony of history willed—as is usual when doctrinaires come to the helm—that both did the opposite of what the doctrines of their school prescribed.

Proudhon, the Socialist of the small peasant and master-craftsman, regarded association with positive hatred. He said of it that there was more bad than good in it; that it was by nature sterile, even harmful, because it was a fetter on the freedom of the worker; that it was a pure dogma, unproductive and burdensome, in conflict as much with the freedom of the worker as with economy of labour; that its disadvantages multiplied more swiftly than its advantages; that, as compared with it, competition, division of labour and private property were economic forces. Only in the exceptional cases—as Proudhon called them—of large-scale industry and large establishments, such as railways, was the association of workers in place. (See *General Idea of the Revolution*, 3rd sketch.)

By 1871, large-scale industry had already so much ceased to be an exceptional case even in Paris, the centre of artistic handicrafts, that by far the most important decree of the Commune instituted an organization of large-scale industry and even of manufacture which was not only to be based on the association of the workers in each factory, but also to combine all these associations in one great union; in short, an organization which, as Marx quite rightly says in *The Civil War*, must necessarily have led in the end to Communism, that is to say, the direct opposite of the Proudhon doctrine. And, therefore, the Commune was the grave of the Proudhon school of Socialism. Today this school has vanished from French working-class circles; here, among the Possibilists [3] no less than among the "Marxists," Marx's theory now rules unchallenged. Only among the "radical" bourgeoisie are there still Proudhonists.

The Blanquists fared no better. Brought up in the school of conspiracy, and held together by the strict discipline which went with it, they started out from the viewpoint that a relatively small number of resolute, well-organized men would be able, at a given favourable moment, not only to seize the helm of state, but also by a display of great, ruthless energy, to maintain power until they succeeded in sweeping the mass of the people into the revolution and ranging them round the small band of leaders. This involved, above all, the strictest, dictatorial centralization of all power in the hands of the new revolutionary government. And what did the Commune, with its majority of these same Blanquists, actually do? In all its proclamations to the French in the provinces, it appealed to them to form a free federation of all French Communes with Paris, a national organization which for the first time was really to be created by the nation itself. It was precisely the oppressing power of the former centralized government, army, political police, bureaucracy, which Napoleon had created in 1798 and which since then had been taken over by every new government as a welcome instrument and used against its opponents—it was precisely this power which was to fall everywhere, just as it had already fallen in Paris.

From the very outset the Commune was compelled to recognize that the working class, once come to power, could not go on managing with the old state machine; that in order not to lose again its only just conquered supremacy, this working class must, on the one hand, do away with all the old repressive machinery previously used against it itself, and, on the other, safeguard itself against its own deputies and officials, by declaring them all, without exception, subject to recall at any moment. What had been the characteristic attribute of the former state? Society had created its own organs to look after its common interests, originally through simple division of labour. But these organs, at whose head was the state power, had in the course of time, in pursuance of their own special interests, transformed themselves from the servants of society into the masters of society. This can be seen, for example, not only in the hereditary monarchy, but equally so in the democratic republic. Nowhere do "politicians" form a more separate and powerful section of the nation than precisely in North America. There, each of the two major parties which alternately succeed each other in power is itself in turn controlled by people who make a business of politics, who speculate on seats in the legislative assemblies of the Union as well as of the separate states, or who make a living by carrying on agitation for their party and on its victory are rewarded with positions. It is well known how the Americans have been trying for thirty years to shake off this yoke, which has become intolerable, and how in spite of it all they continue to sink ever deeper in this swamp of corruption. It is precisely in America that we see best how there takes place this process of the state power making itself independent in relation to society, whose mere instrument it was originally intended to be. Here there exists no dynasty, no nobility, no standing army, beyond the few men keeping watch on the Indians, no bureaucracy with permanent posts or the right to pen-sions. And nevertheless we find here two great gangs of political speculators, who alternately take possession of the state power and exploit it by the most corrupt means and for the most corrupt ends—and the nation is powerless against these two great cartels of politicians, who are ostensibly its servants, but in reality dominate and plunder it.

Against this transformation of the state and the organs of the state from servants of society into masters of society —an inevitable transformation in all previous states—the Commune made use of two infallible means. In the first place, it filled all posts—administrative, judicial and educational—by election on the basis of universal suffrage of all concerned, subject to the right of recall at any time by the same electors. And, in the second place, all officials, high or low, were paid only the wages received by other workers. The highest salary paid by the Commune to anyone was 6,000 francs. In this way an effective barrier to place-hunting and careerism was set up, even apart from the binding mandates to delegates to representative bodies which were added besides.

This shattering [*Sprengung*] of the former state power and its replacement by a new and truly democratic one is described in detail in the third section of *The Civil War*. But it was necessary to dwell briefly here once more on some of its features, because in Germany particularly the superstitious belief in the state has been carried over from philosophy into the general consciousness of the bourgeoisie and even of many workers. According to the philosophical conception, the state is the "realization of the idea," or the Kingdom of God on earth, translated into philosophical terms, the sphere in which eternal truth and justice is or should be realized. And from this follows a superstitious reverence for the state and everything connected with it, which takes root the more readily since people are accustomed from childhood to imagine that the affairs and interests common to the whole of society could not be looked after otherwise than as they have been looked after in the past, that is, through the state and its lucratively positioned officials. And people think they have taken quite an extraordinarily bold step forward when they have rid themselves of belief in hereditary monarchy and swear by the democratic republic. In reality, however, the state is nothing but a machine for the oppression of one class by another, and indeed in the democratic republic no less than in the monarchy; and at best an evil inherited by the proletariat after its victorious struggle for class supremacy, whose worst sides the victorious proletariat, just like the Commune, cannot avoid having to lop off at once as much as possible until such time as a generation reared in new, free social conditions is able to throw the entire lumber of the state on the scrap heap.

Of late, the Social-Democratic philistine has once more been filled with wholesome terror at the words: Dictatorship of the Proletariat. Well and good, gentlemen, do you want to know what this dictatorship looks like? Look at the Paris Commune. That was the Dictatorship of the Proletariat.

F. Engels

London, on the twentieth anniversary of the Paris Commune, March 18, 1891

Translated from the German

Written by Engels for the separate edition of Marx's *The Civil War in France,* Berlin, 1891

FIRST ADDRESS OF THE GENERAL COUNCIL OF THE INTERNATIONAL WORKING MEN'S ASSOCIATION ON THE FRANCO-PRUSSIAN WAR

To the Members of the International Working Men's Association in Europe and the United States

In the Inaugural Address of the *International Working Men's Association,* of November, 1864, we said:—"If the emancipation of the working classes requires their fraternal concurrence, how are they to fulfil that great mission with a foreign policy in pursuit of criminal designs, playing upon national prejudices and squandering in piratical wars the people's blood and treasure?" We defined the foreign policy aimed at by the International in these words: "Vindicate the simple laws of morals and justice, which ought to govern the relations of private individuals, as the laws paramount of the intercourse of nations."

No wonder that Louis Bonaparte, who usurped his power by exploiting the war of classes in France, and perpetuated it by periodical wars abroad, should from the first have treated the International as a dangerous foe. On the eve of the plebiscite [4] he ordered a raid on the members of the Administrative Committees of the International Working Men's Association throughout France, at Paris, Lyons, Rouen, Marseilles, Brest, etc., on the pretext that the International was a secret society dabbling in a complot for his assassination, a pretext soon after exposed in its full absurdity by his own judges. What was the real crime of the French branches of the International? They told the French people publicly and emphatically that voting the plebiscite was voting despotism at home and war abroad. It has been, in fact, their work that in all the great towns, in all the industrial centres of France, the working class rose like one man to reject the plebiscite. Unfortunately the balance was turned by the heavy ignorance of the rural districts. The Stock Exchanges, the Cabinets, the ruling classes and the press of Europe celebrated the plebiscite as a signal victory of the French Emperor over the French working class; and it was the signal for the assassination, not of an individual, but of nations.

The war plot of July, 1870, is but an amended edition of the *coup d'état* of December, 1851.[5] At first view the thing seemed so absurd that France would not believe in its real good earnest. It rather believed the deputy denouncing the ministerial war talk as a mere stock-jobbing trick. When, on July 15th, war was at last officially announced to the *Corps Législatif*, the whole opposition refused to vote the preliminary subsidies, even Thiers branded it as "detestable"; all the independent journals of Paris condemned it, and, wonderful to relate, the provincial press joined in almost unanimously.

Meanwhile, the Paris members of the International had again set to work. In the *Réveil*[6] of July 12th they published their manifesto "to the workmen of all nations," from which we extract the following few passages:

"Once more," they say, "on the pretext of the European equilibrium, of national honour, the peace of the world is menaced by political ambitions. French, German, Spanish workmen! let our voices unite in one cry of reprobation against war!... War for a question of preponderance or a dynasty, can, in the eyes of workmen, be nothing but a criminal absurdity. In answer to the warlike proclamations of those who exempt themselves from the impost of blood, and find in public misfortunes a source of fresh speculations, we protest, we who want peace, labour and liberty!... Brothers of Germany! Our division would only result in the complete triumph *of despotism* on both sides of the Rhine.... Workmen of all countries! whatever may for the present become of our common efforts, we, the members of the International Working Men's Association, who know of no frontiers, we send you as a pledge of indissoluble solidarity the good wishes and the salutations of the workmen of France."

This manifesto of our Paris section was followed by numerous similar French addresses, of which we can here only quote the declaration of Neuilly-sur-Seine, published in the *Marseillaise*[7] of July 22nd: "The war, is it just?—No! The war, is it national?—No! It is merely dynastic. In the name of humanity, of democracy, and the true interests of France, we adhere completely and energetically to the protestation of the International against the war."

These protestations expressed the true sentiments of the French working people, as was soon shown by a curious incident. *The Band of the 10th of December*,[8] first organized under the presidency of Louis Bonaparte, having been masqueraded into *blouses* and let loose on the streets of Paris, there to perform the contortions of war fever, the real workmen of the Faubourgs came forward with public peace demonstrations so overwhelming that Pietri, the Prefect of Police, thought it prudent to at once stop all further street politics, on the plea that the real Paris people had given sufficient vent to their pent up patriotism and exuberant war enthusiasm.

Whatever may be the incidents of Louis Bonaparte's war with Prussia, the death knell of the Second Empire has already sounded at Paris. It will end as it began, by a parody. But let us not forget that it is the Governments and the ruling classes of Europe who enabled Louis Bonaparte to play during eighteen years the ferocious farce of the *Restored Empire*.

On the German side, the war is a war of defence, but who put Germany to the necessity of defending herself? Who enabled Louis Bonaparte to wage war upon her? *Prussia!* It was Bismarck who conspired with that very same Louis Bonaparte for the purpose of crushing popular opposition at home, and annexing Germany to the Hohenzollern dynasty. If the battle of Sadowa[9] had been lost instead of being won, French battalions would have overrun Germany as the allies of Prussia. After her victory, did Prussia dream one moment of opposing a free Germany to an enslaved France? Just the contrary. While carefully preserving all the native beauties of her old system, she superadded all the tricks of the Second Empire, its real despotism and its mock democratism, its political shams and its financial jobs, its high-flown talk and its low *legerdemains*. The Bonapartist regime, which till then only flourished on one side of the Rhine, had now got its counterfeit on the other. From such a state of things, what else could result but *war*?

If the German working class allow the present war to lose its strictly defensive character and to degenerate into a war against the French people, victory or defeat will prove alike disastrous. All the miseries that befell Germany after her war of independence [10] will revive with accumulated intensity.

The principles of the International are, however, too widely spread and too firmly rooted amongst the German working class to apprehend such a sad consummation. The voices of the French workmen have re-echoed from Germany. A mass meeting of workmen, held at Brunswick on July 16th, expressed its full concurrence with the Paris manifesto, spurned the idea of national antagonism to France, and wound up its resolutions with these words:— "We are enemies of all wars, but above all of dynastic wars.... With deep sorrow and grief we are forced to undergo a defensive war as an unavoidable evil; but we call, at the same time, upon the whole German working class to render the recurrence of such an immense social misfortune impossible by vindicating for the peoples themselves the power to decide on peace and war, and making them masters of their own destinies."

At Chemnitz, a meeting of delegates representing 50,000 Saxon workers adopted unanimously a resolution to this effect:—"In the name of the German Democracy, and especially of the workmen forming the Democratic Socialist party, we declare the present war to be exclusively dynastic.... We are happy to grasp the fraternal hand stretched out to us by the workmen of France.... Mindful of the watchword of the International Working Men's Association: *Proletarians of all countries, unite*, we shall never forget that the workmen of *all* countries are our *friends* and the despots of *all* countries our *enemies*." The Berlin branch of the International has also replied to the Paris manifesto:—"We," they say, "join with heart and hand your protestation.... Solemnly we promise that neither the sound of the trumpet, nor the roar of the cannon, neither victory nor defeat shall divert us from our common work for the union of the children of toil of all countries."

Be it so!

In the background of this suicidal strife looms the dark figure of Russia. It is an ominous sign that the signal for the present war should have been given at the moment when the Moscovite Government had just finished its strategical lines of railway and was already massing troops in the direction of the Pruth. Whatever sympathy the Germans may justly claim in a war of defence against Bonapartist aggression, they would forfeit at once by allowing the Prussian Government to call for, or accept, the help of the Cossack. Let them remember that, after their war of independence against the first Napoleon, Germany lay for generations prostrate at the feet of the Czar.

The English working class stretch the hand of fellowship to the French and German working people. They feel deeply convinced that whatever turn the impending horrid war may take, the alliance of the working classes of all countries will ultimately kill war. The very fact that while official France and Germany are rushing into a fratricidal feud, the workmen of France and Germany send each other messages of peace and goodwill; this great fact, unparalleled in the history of the past, opens the vista of a brighter future. It proves that in contrast to old society, with its economical miseries and its political delirium, a new society is springing up, whose International rule will be *Peace*, because its national ruler will be everywhere the same—*Labour*! The Pioneer of that new society is the International Working Men's Association.

London, July 23, 1870

Written by Marx and endorsed at a session of the General Council of the International Working Men's Association held on July 23, 1870

Printed forthwith, in the form of leaflets, in English, German and French

Printed according to the text of the English leaflet

SECOND ADDRESS OF THE GENERAL COUNCIL OF THE INTERNATIONAL WORKING MEN'S ASSOCIATION ON THE FRANCO-PRUSSIAN WAR

To the Members of the International Working Men's Association in Europe and the United States

In our first Manifesto of the 23rd of July we said:—"The death knell of the Second Empire has already sounded at Paris. It will end as it began, by a parody. But let us not forget that it is the Governments and the ruling classes of Europe who enabled Louis Napoleon to play during eighteen years the ferocious farce of the *Restored Empire*."

Thus, even before war operations had actually set in, we treated the Bonapartist bubble as a thing of the past.

If we were not mistaken as to the vitality of the Second Empire, we were not wrong in our apprehension lest the German war should "lose its strictly defensive character and degenerate into a war against the French people." The war of defence ended, in point of fact, with the surrender of Louis Bonaparte, the Sedan capitulation, and the proclamation of the Republic at Paris.[11] But long before these events, the very moment that the utter rottenness of the Imperialist arms became evident, the Prussian military *camarilla* had resolved upon conquest. There lay an ugly obstacle in their way—*King William's own proclamations at the commencement of the war*. In his speech from the throne to the North German Diet, he had solemnly declared to make war upon the emperor of the French, and not upon the French people. On the 11th of August he had issued a manifesto to the French nation, where he said: "The Emperor Napoleon having made, by land and sea, an attack on the German nation, which desired and still desires to live in peace with the French people, I have assumed the command of the German armies *to repel his aggression*, and I have been led by *military events to cross the frontiers of France.*" Not content to assert the defensive character of the war by the statement that he only assumed the command of the German armies "*to repel aggression*," he added that he was only "led by military events" to cross the frontiers of France. A defensive war does, of course, not exclude offensive operations, dictated by "military events."

Thus this pious king stood pledged before France and the world to a strictly defensive war. How to release him from his solemn pledge? The stage-managers had to exhibit him as giving, reluctantly, way to the irresistible behest of the German nation. They at once gave the cue to the liberal German middle class, with its professors, its capitalists, its aldermen, and its penmen. That middle class which in its struggle for civil liberty had, from 1846 to 1870, been exhibiting an unexampled spectacle of irresolution, incapacity, and cowardice, felt, of course, highly delighted to bestride the European scene as the roaring lion of German patriotism. It re-vindicated its civic independence by affecting to force upon the Prussian Government the secret designs of that same government. It does penance for its long-continued and almost religious faith in Louis Bonaparte's infallibility, by shouting for the dismemberment of the French Republic. Let us for a moment listen to the special pleadings of those stout-hearted patriots!

They dare not pretend that the people of Alsace and Lorraine pant for the German embrace; quite the contrary. To punish their French patriotism, Strasburg, a town with an independent citadel commanding it, has for six days been wantonly and fiendishly bombarded by "German" explosive shells, setting it on fire, and killing great numbers of its defenceless inhabitants! Yet, the soil of those provinces once upon a time belonged to the whilom German Empire. Hence, it seems, the soil and the human beings grown on it must be confiscated as imprescriptible German property. If the map of Europe is to be remade in the antiquary's vein, let us by no means forget that the Elector of Brandenburg, for his Prussian dominions, was the vassal of the Polish Republic.

The more knowing patriots, however, require Alsace and the German-speaking part of Lorraine as a "material guarantee" against French aggression. As this contemptible plea has bewildered many weak-minded people, we are bound to enter more fully upon it.

There is no doubt that the general configuration of Alsace, as compared with the opposite bank of the Rhine, and the presence of a large fortified town like Strasburg, about halfway between Basle and Germersheim, very much favour a French invasion of South Germany, while they offer peculiar difficulties to an invasion of France from South Germany. There is, further, no doubt that the addition of Alsace and German-speaking Lorraine would give South Germany a much stronger frontier, inasmuch as she would then be master of the crest of the Vosges mountains in its whole length, and of the fortresses which cover its northern passes. If Metz were annexed as well, France would certainly for the moment be deprived of her two principal bases of operation against Germany, but that would not prevent her from constructing a fresh one at Nancy or Verdun. While Germany owns Coblentz, Mainz, Germersheim, Rastadt, and Ulm, all bases of operation against France, and plentifully made use of in this war, with what show of fair play can she begrudge France Strasburg and Metz, the only two fortresses of any importance she has on that side? Moreover, Strasburg endangers South Germany only while South Germany is a separate power from North Germany. From 1792-95 South Germany was never invaded from that direction, because Prussia was a party to the war against the French Revolution; but as soon as Prussia made a peace of her own in 1795, and left the South to shift for itself, the invasions of South Germany with Strasburg for a base, began, and continued till 1809. The fact is, a *united* Germany can always render Strasburg and any French army in Alsace innocuous by concentrating all her troops, as was done in the present war, between Saarlouis and Landau, and advancing, or accepting battle, on the line of road between Mainz and Metz. While the mass of the German troops is stationed there, any French army advancing from Strasburg into South Germany would be outflanked, and have its communications threatened. If the present campaign has proved anything, it is the facility of invading France from Germany.

But, in good faith, is it not altogether an absurdity and an anachronism to make military considerations the principle by which the boundaries of nations are to be fixed? If this rule were to prevail, Austria would still be entitled to Venetia and the line of the Mincio, and France to the line of the Rhine, in order to protect Paris, which lies certainly more open to an attack from the North East than Berlin does from the South West. If limits are to be fixed by military interests, there will be no end to claims, because every military line is necessarily faulty, and may be improved by annexing some more outlying territory; and, moreover, they can never be fixed finally and fairly, because they always must be imposed by the conqueror upon the conquered, and consequently carry within them the seed of fresh wars.

Such is the lesson of all history. Thus with nations as with individuals. To deprive them of the power of offence, you must deprive them of the means of defence. You must not only garotte but murder. If ever conqueror took "material guarantees" for breaking the sinews of a nation, the first Napoleon did so by the Tilsit treaty,[12] and the way he executed it against Prussia and the rest of Germany. Yet, a few years later, his gigantic power split like a rotten reed upon the German people. What are the "material guarantees" Prussia, in her wildest dreams, can, or dare impose upon France, compared to the "material guarantees" the first Napoleon had wrenched from herself? The result will not prove the less disastrous. History will measure its retribution, not by the extent of the square miles conquered from France, but by the intensity of the crime of reviving, in the second half of the 19th century, *the policy of conquest!*

But, say the mouthpieces of Teutonic patriotism, you must not confound Germans with Frenchmen. What we want is not glory, but safety. The Germans are an essentially peaceful people. In their sober guardianship, conquest itself changes from a condition of future war into a pledge of perpetual peace. Of course, it is not Germans that invaded France in 1792, for the sublime purpose of bayoneting the revolution of the 18th century. It is not

Germans that befouled their hands by the subjugation of Italy, the oppression of Hungary, and the dismemberment of Poland. Their present military system, which divides the whole adult male population into two parts,—one standing army on service, and another standing army on furlough, both equally bound in passive obedience to rulers by divine right,—such a military system is, of course, a "material guarantee" for keeping the peace, and the ultimate goal of civilizing tendencies! In Germany, as everywhere else, the sycophants of the powers that be poison the popular mind by the incense of mendacious self-praise.

Indignant as they pretend to be at the sight of French fortresses in Metz and Strasburg, those German patriots see no harm in the vast system of Moscovite fortifications at Warsaw, Modlin, and Ivangorod. While gloating at the terrors of imperialist invasion, they blink at the infamy of autocratic tutelage.

As in 1865 promises were exchanged between Louis Bonaparte and Bismarck, so in 1870 promises have been exchanged between Gorchakov and Bismarck. As Louis Bonaparte flattered himself that the War of 1866, resulting in the common exhaustion of Austria and Prussia, would make him the supreme arbiter of Germany, so Alexander flattered himself that the War of 1870, resulting in the common exhaustion of Germany and France, would make him the supreme arbiter of the Western Continent. As the Second Empire thought the North German Confederation incompatible with its existence, so autocratic Russia must think herself endangered by a German empire under Prussian leadership. Such is the law of the old political system. Within its pale the gain of one state is the loss of the other. The Czar's paramount influence over Europe roots in his traditional hold on Germany. At a moment when in Russia herself volcanic social agencies threaten to shake the very base of autocracy, could the Czar afford to bear with such a loss of foreign prestige? Already the Moscovite journals repeat the language of the Bonapartist journals after the War of 1866. Do the Teuton patriots really believe that liberty and peace will be guaranteed to Germany by forcing France into the arms of Russia? If the fortune of her arms, the arrogance of success, and dynastic intrigue lead Germany to a dismemberment of France, there will then only remain two courses open to her. She must at all risks become the *avowed* tool of Russian aggrandizement, or, after some short respite, make again ready for another "defensive" war, not one of those new-fangled "localized" wars, but a *war of races*—a war with the combined Slavonian and Roman races.

The German working class has resolutely supported the war, which it was not in their power to prevent, as a war for German independence and the liberation of France and Europe from that pestilential incubus, the Second Empire. It was the German workmen who, together with the rural labourers, furnished the sinews and muscles of heroic hosts, leaving behind their half-starved families. Decimated by the battles abroad, they will be once more decimated by misery at home. In their turn they are now coming forward to ask for "guarantees,"—guarantees that their immense sacrifices have not been brought in vain, that they have conquered liberty, that the victory over the Imperialist armies will not, as in 1815, be turned into the defeat of the German people; and, as the first of these guarantees, they claim an *honourable peace for France*, and the *recognition of the French Republic*.

The Central Committee of the German Socialist-Democratic Workmen's Party issued, on the 5th of September, a manifesto, energetically insisting upon these guarantees. "We," they say, "we protest against the annexation of Alsace and Lorraine. And we are conscious of speaking in the name of the German working class. In the common interest of France and Germany, in the interest of peace and liberty, in the interest of Western civilization against Eastern barbarism, the German workmen will not patiently tolerate the annexation of Alsace and Lorraine. . . . We shall faithfully stand by our fellow-workmen in all countries for the common international cause of the Proletariat!"

Unfortunately, we cannot feel sanguine of their immediate success. If the French workmen amidst peace failed to stop the aggressor, are the German workmen more likely to stop the victor amidst the clangour of arms? The German workmen's manifesto demands the extradition of Louis Bonaparte as a common felon to the French Republic. Their rulers are, on the contrary, already trying hard to restore him to the Tuileries as the best man to ruin France. However that may be, history will prove that the German working class are not made of the same malleable stuff as the German middle class. They will do their duty.

Like them, we hail the advent of the Republic in France, but at the same time we labour under misgivings which we hope will prove groundless. That Republic has not subverted the throne, but only taken its place become vacant. It has been proclaimed, not as a social conquest, but as a national measure of defence. It is in the hands of a Provisional Government composed partly of notorious Orleanists, partly of middle-class Republicans, upon some of whom the insurrection of June, 1848, has left its indelible stigma. The division of labour amongst the members of that Government looks awkward. The Orleanists have seized the strongholds of the army and the police, while to the professed Republicans have fallen the talking departments. Some of their first acts go far to show that they have inherited from the Empire, not only ruins, but also its dread of the working class. If eventual impossibilities are in wild phraseology demanded from the Republic, is it not with a view to prepare the cry for a "possible" government? Is the Republic, by some of its middle-class managers, not intended to serve as a mere stopgap and bridge over an Orleanist Restoration?

The French working class moves, therefore, under circumstances of extreme difficulty. Any attempt at upsetting the new Government in the present crisis, when the enemy is almost knocking at the doors of Paris, would be a desperate folly. The French workmen must perform their duties as citizens; but, at the same time, they must not allow themselves to be deluded by the national *souvenirs** of 1792, as the French peasants allowed themselves to be deluded by the national *souvenirs* of the First Empire. They have not to recapitulate the past, but to build up the future. Let them calmly and resolutely improve the opportunities of Republican liberty, for the work of their own class organization. It will gift them with fresh Her-

---

* Traditions.—*Ed.*

culean powers for the regeneration of France, and our common task—the emancipation of labour. Upon their energies and wisdom hinges the fate of the Republic.

The English workmen have already taken measures to overcome, by a wholesome pressure from without, the reluctance of their Government to recognize the French Republic.[13] The present dilatoriness of the British Government is probably intended to atone for the Anti-Jacobin war and its former indecent haste in sanctioning the *coup d'état*. The English workmen call also upon their Government to oppose by all its power the dismemberment of France, which part of the English press is so shameless enough to howl for. It is the same press that for twenty years deified Louis Bonaparte as the providence of Europe, that frantically cheered on the slaveholders' rebellion.[14] Now, as then, it drudges for the slaveholder.

Let the sections of the *International Working Men's Association* in every country stir the working classes to action. If they forsake their duty, if they remain passive, the present tremendous war will be but the harbinger of still deadlier international feuds, and lead in every nation to a renewed triumph over the workman by the lords of the sword, of the soil, and of capital.

Vive la République.

Written by Marx and endorsed at a session of the General Council of the International Working Men's Association held on September 9, 1870

Printed at once, in the form of leaflets, in English, German and French

Printed according to the text of the English leaflet

ADDRESS OF THE GENERAL COUNCIL OF THE INTERNATIONAL WORKING MEN'S ASSOCIATION ON THE CIVIL WAR IN FRANCE, 1871

To All the Members of the Association in Europe and the United States

I

On the 4th of September, 1870, when the working men of Paris proclaimed the Republic, which was almost instantaneously acclaimed throughout France, without a single voice of dissent, a cabal of place-hunting barristers, with Thiers for their statesman and Trochu for their general, took hold of the Hôtel de Ville. At that time they were imbued with so fanatical a faith in the mission of Paris to represent France in all epochs of historical crisis, that, to legitimate their usurped titles as governors of France, they thought it quite sufficient to produce their lapsed mandates as representatives of Paris. In our second address on the late war, five days after the rise of these men, we told you who they were. Yet, in the turmoil of surprise, with the real leaders of the working class still shut up in Bonapartist prisons and the Prussians already marching upon Paris, Paris bore with their assumption of power, on the express condition that it was to be wielded for the single purpose of national defence. Paris, however, was not to be defended without arming its working class, organizing them into an effective force, and training their ranks by the war itself. But Paris armed was the Revolution armed. A victory of Paris over the Prussian aggressor would have been a victory of the French workman over the French capitalist and his State parasites. In this conflict between national duty and class interest, the Government of National Defence did not hesitate one moment to turn into a Government of National Defection.

The first step they took was to send Thiers on a roving tour to all the courts of Europe, there to beg mediation by offering the barter of the Republic for a king. Four months after the commencement of the siege, when they thought the opportune moment come for breaking the first word of capitulation, Trochu, in the presence of Jules Favre and others of his colleagues, addressed the assembled mayors of Paris in these terms:

"The first question put to me by my colleagues on the very evening of the 4th of September was this: Paris, can it with any chance of success stand a siege by the Prussian army? I did not hesitate to answer in the negative. Some of my colleagues here present will warrant the truth of my words and the persistence of my opinion. I told them, in these very terms, that, under the existing state of things, the attempt of Paris to hold out a siege by the Prussian army would be a folly. Without doubt, I added, it would be an heroic folly; but that would be all.... The events (managed by himself) have not given the lie to my prevision."

This nice little speech of Trochu was afterwards published by M. Corbon, one of the mayors present.

Thus, on the very evening of the proclamation of the republic, Trochu's "plan" was known to his colleagues to be the capitulation of Paris. If national defence had been more than a pretext for the personal government of Thiers, Favre, and Co., the upstarts of the 4th of September would have abdicated on the 5th—would have initiated the Paris people into Trochu's "plan," and called upon them to surrender at once, or to take their own fate into their own hands. Instead of this, the infamous impostors resolved upon curing the heroic folly of Paris by a regimen of famine and broken heads, and to dupe her in the meanwhile by ranting manifestoes, holding forth that Trochu, "the governor of Paris, will never capitulate," and Jules Favre, the foreign minister, will "not cede an inch of our territory, nor a stone of our fortresses." In a letter to Gambetta, that very same Jules Favre avows that what they were "defending" against was not the Prussian soldiers, but the working men of Paris. During the whole continuance of the siege the Bonapartist cut-throats, whom Trochu had wisely intrusted with the command of the Paris army, exchanged, in their intimate correspondence, ribald jokes at the well-understood mockery of defence. (See, for instance, the correspondence of Alphonse Simon Guiod, supreme commander of the artillery of the Army of Defence of Paris and Grand Cross of the Legion of Honour, to Susanne, general of division of artillery, a correspondence published by the *Journal Officiel* [15] of the Commune.) The mask of imposture was at last dropped on the 28th of January, 1871. With the true heroism of utter self-debasement, the Government of National Defence, in their capitulation, came out as the government of France by Bismarck's prisoners —a part so base that Louis Bonaparte himself had, at Sedan, shrunk from accepting it. After the events of the 18th of March, on their wild flight to Versailles, the *capitulards* left in the hands of Paris the documentary evidence of their treason, to destroy which, as the Commune says in its manifesto to the provinces, "those men would not recoil from battering Paris into a heap of ruins washed by a sea of blood."

To be eagerly bent upon such a consummation, some of the leading members of the Government of Defence had, besides, most peculiar reasons of their own.

Shortly after the conclusion of the armistice, M. Millière, one of the representatives of Paris to the National Assembly, now shot by express order of Jules Favre, published a series of authentic legal documents in proof that Jules Favre, living in concubinage with the wife of a drunkard resident at Algiers, had, by a most daring concoction of forgeries, spread over many years, contrived to grasp, in the name of the children of his adultery, a large succession, which made him a rich man, and that, in a lawsuit undertaken by the legitimate heirs, he only escaped exposure by the connivance of the Bonapartist tribunals. As these dry legal documents were not to be got rid of by any amount of rhetorical horse-power, Jules Favre, for the first time in his life, held his tongue, quietly awaiting the outbreak of the civil war, in order, then, frantically to denounce the people of Paris as a band of escaped convicts in utter revolt against family, religion, order and property. This same forger had hardly got into power, after the 4th of September, when he sympathetically let loose upon society Pic and Taillefer, convicted, even under the empire, of forgery, in the scandalous affair of the *Étendard*.[16] One of these men, Taillefer, having dared to return to Paris under the Commune, was at once reinstated in prison; and then Jules Favre exclaimed, from the tribune of the National Assembly, that Paris was setting free all her jailbirds!

Ernest Picard, the Joe Miller [17] of the Government of National Defence, who appointed himself Finance Minister of the Republic after having in vain striven to become the Home Minister of the Empire, is the brother of one Arthur Picard, an individual expelled from the Paris *Bourse* as a blackleg (see report of the Prefecture of Police, dated the 13th of July, 1867), and convicted, on his own confession, of a theft of 300,000 francs, while manager of one of the branches of the *Société Générale*, rue Palestro, No. 5 (see report of the Prefecture of Police, 11th December, 1868). This Arthur Picard was made by Ernest Picard the editor of his paper, *l'Electeur Libre*. While the common run of stockjobbers were led astray by the official lies of this Finance Office paper, Arthur was running backwards and forwards between the Finance Office and the *Bourse*, there to discount the disasters of the French army. The whole financial correspondence of that worthy pair of brothers fell into the hands of the Commune.

Jules Ferry, a penniless barrister before the 4th of September, contrived, as Mayor of Paris during the siege, to job a fortune out of famine. The day on which he would have to give an account of his maladministration would be the day of his conviction.

These men, then, could find, in the ruins of Paris only, their tickets-of-leave: they were the very men Bismarck wanted. With the help of some shuffling of cards, Thiers, hitherto the secret prompter of the Government, now appeared at its head, with the ticket-of-leave-men* for his Ministers.

Thiers, that monstrous gnome, has charmed the French bourgeoisie for almost half a century, because he is the most consummate intellectual expression of their own class-corruption. Before he became a statesman he had already proved his lying powers as an historian. The chronicle of his public life is the record of the misfortunes of France. Banded, before 1830, with the Republicans, he slipped into office under Louis Philippe by betraying his protector Laffitte, ingratiating himself with the king by exciting mob-riots against the clergy, during which the church of Saint Germain l'Auxerrois and the Archbishop's palace were plundered, and by acting the minister-spy upon, and the jail-*accoucheur* of, the Duchess de Berry. The massacre of the republicans in the rue Transnonain, and the subsequent infamous laws of September against the press and the right of association, were his work. Reappearing as the chief of the Cabinet in March, 1840, he astonished France with his plan of fortifying Paris. To the Republicans, who denounced this plan as a sinister plot against the liberty of Paris, he replied from the tribune of the Chamber of Deputies:

"What! to fancy that any works of fortification could ever endanger liberty! And first of all you calumniate any possible Government in supposing that it could some day attempt to maintain itself by bombarding the capital; ..but that government would be a hundred times more impossible after its victory than before." Indeed, no Government would ever have dared to bombard Paris from the forts, but that Government which had previously surrendered these forts to the Prussians.

When King Bomba tried his hand at Palermo, in January, 1848, Thiers, then long since out of office, again rose in the Chamber of Deputies: "You know, gentlemen,

---

* In England common criminals are often discharged on parole after serving the greater part of their term, and are placed under police surveillance. On such discharge they receive a certificate called ticket-of-leave, their possessors being referred to as ticket-of-leave-men. [*Note by Engels to the German edition of 1871.*]

38

what is happening at Palermo. [18] You, all of you, shake with horror (in the parliamentary sense) on hearing that during forty-eight hours a large town has been bombarded —by whom? Was it by a foreign enemy exercising the rights of war? No, gentlemen, it was by its own Government. And why? Because that unfortunate town demanded its rights. Well, then, for the demand of its rights it has got forty-eight hours of bombardment.... Allow me to appeal to the opinion of Europe. It is doing a service to mankind to arise, and to make reverberate, from what is perhaps the greatest tribune in Europe, some words (indeed words) of indignation against such acts.... When the Regent Espartero, who had rendered services to his country (which M. Thiers never did), intended bombarding Barcelona, in order to suppress its insurrection, there arose from all parts of the world a general outcry of indignation."

Eighteen months afterwards, M. Thiers was amongst the fiercest defenders of the bombardment of Rome by a French army. [19] In fact, the fault of King Bomba seems to have consisted in this only, that he limited his bombardment to forty-eight hours.

A few days before the Revolution of February, fretting at the long exile from place and pelf to which Guizot had condemned him, and sniffing in the air the scent of an approaching popular commotion, Thiers, in that pseudo-heroic style which won him the nickname of *Mirabeau-mouche*,* declared to the Chamber of Deputies: "I am of the party of Revolution, not only in France, but in Europe. I wish the Government of the Revolution to remain in the hands of moderate men... but if that Government should fall into the hands of ardent minds, even into those of Radicals, I shall, for all that, not desert my cause. I shall always be of the party of the Revolution." The Revolution of February came. Instead of displacing the Guizot Cabinet by the Thiers Cabinet, as the little man had dreamt, it superseded Louis Philippe by the Republic. On the first day of the popular victory he carefully hid himself, forgetting that the contempt of the working men screened him from their hatred. Still, with his legendary

---

* Mirabeau the fly.—*Ed*.

courage, he continued to shy the public stage, until the June massacres * had cleared it for his sort of action. Then he became the leading mind of the "Party of Order" [20] and its Parliamentary Republic, that anonymous interregnum, in which all the rival factions of the ruling class conspired together to crush the people, and conspired against each other to restore each of them its own monarchy. Then, as now, Thiers denounced the Republicans as the only obstacle to the consolidation of the Republic; then, as now, he spoke to the Republic as the hangman spoke to Don Carlos:—"I shall assassinate thee, but for thy own good." Now, as then, he will have to exclaim on the day after his victory: *"L'Empire est fait"*—the Empire is consummated. Despite his hypocritical homilies about necessary liberties and his personal grudge against Louis Bonaparte, who had made a dupe of him, and kicked out parliamentarism —and outside of its factitious atmosphere the little man is conscious of withering into nothingness—he had a hand in all the infamies of the Second Empire, from the occupation of Rome by French troops to the war with Prussia, which he incited by his fierce invective against German unity—not as a cloak of Prussian despotism, but as an encroachment upon the vested right of France in German disunion. Fond of brandishing, with his dwarfish arms, in the face of Europe the sword of the first Napoleon, whose historical shoe-black he had become, his foreign policy always culminated in the utter humiliation of France, from the London convention of 1840 to the Paris capitulation of 1871, and the present civil war, where he hounds on the prisoners of Sedan and Metz against Paris by special permission of Bismarck. Despite his versatility of talent and shiftness of purpose, this man has his whole lifetime been wedded to the most fossil routine. It is self-evident that to him the deeper under-currents of modern society remained forever hidden; but even the most palpable changes on its surface were abhorrent to a brain all the vitality of which had fled to the tongue. Thus he never tired of denouncing as a sacrilege any deviation from the old French protective system. When a minister of Louis Philippe, he railed at railways as a wild chimera; and when in opposi-

---

* This refers to the suppression of the June insurrection of the Paris proletariat in 1848.—*Ed.*

tion under Louis Bonaparte, he branded as a profanation every attempt to reform the rotten French army system. Never in his long political career has he been guilty of a single—even the smallest—measure of any practical use. Thiers was consistent only in his greed for wealth and his hatred of the men that produce it. Having entered his first ministry under Louis Philippe poor as Job, he left it a millionaire. His last ministry under the same king (of the 1st of March, 1840) exposed him to public taunts of peculation in the Chamber of Deputies, to which he was content to reply by tears—a commodity he deals in as freely as Jules Favre, or any other crocodile. At Bordeaux his first measure for saving France from impending financial ruin was to endow himself with three millions a year, the first and the last word of the "Economical Republic," the vista of which he had opened to his Paris electors in 1869. One of his former colleagues of the Chamber of Deputies of 1830, himself a capitalist and, nevertheless, a devoted member of the Paris Commune, M. Beslay, lately addressed Thiers thus in a public placard: "The enslavement of labour by capital has always been the corner-stone of your policy, and from the very day you saw the Republic of Labour installed at the Hôtel de Ville, you have never ceased to cry out to France: 'These are criminals!'" A master in small state roguery, a virtuoso in perjury and treason, a craftsman in all the petty stratagems, cunning devices, and base perfidies of parliamentary party-warfare; never scrupling, when out of office, to fan a revolution, and to stifle it in blood when at the helm of the state; with class prejudices standing him in the place of ideas, and vanity in the place of a heart; his private life as infamous as his public life is odious—even now, when playing the part of a French Sulla, he cannot help setting off the abomination of his deeds by the ridicule of his ostentation.

The capitulation of Paris, by surrendering to Prussia not only Paris, but all France, closed the long-continued intrigues of treason with the enemy, which the usurpers of the 4th of September had begun, as Trochu himself said, on that very same day. On the other hand, it initiated the civil war they were now to wage, with the assistance of Prussia, against the Republic and Paris. The trap was laid in the very terms of the capitulation. At that time above one-third of the territory was in the hands of the enemy, the capital was cut off from the provinces, all communications were disorganized. To elect under such circumstances a real representation of France was impossible, unless ample time were given for preparation. In view of this, the capitulation stipulated that a National Assembly must be elected within eight days; so that in many parts of France the news of the impending election arrived on its eve only. This assembly, moreover, was, by an express clause of the capitulation, to be elected for the sole purpose of deciding on peace or war, and, eventually, to conclude a treaty of peace. The population could not but feel that the terms of the armistice rendered the continuation of the war impossible, and that for sanctioning the peace imposed by Bismarck, the worst men in France were the best. But not content with these precautions, Thiers, even before the secret of the armistice had been broached to Paris, set out for an electioneering tour through the provinces, there to galvanize back into life the Legitimist party, which now, along with the Orleanists, [21] had to take the place of the then impossible Bonapartists. He was not afraid of them. Impossible as a government of modern France, and, therefore, contemptible as rivals, what party were more eligible as tools of counter-revolution than the party whose action, in the words of Thiers himself (Chamber of Deputies, 5th January, 1833), "had always been confined to the three resources of foreign invasion, civil war, and anarchy"? They verily believed in the advent of their long-expected retrospective millennium. There were the heels of foreign invasion trampling upon France; there was the downfall of an empire, and the captivity of a Bonaparte; and there they were themselves. The wheel of history had evidently rolled back to stop at the "Chambre introuvable" [22] of 1816. In the assemblies of the republic, 1848 to 1851, they had been represented by their educated and trained parliamentary champions; it was the rank-and-file of the party which now rushed in—all the Pourceaugnacs [23] of France.

As soon as this Assembly of "Rurals" [24] had met at Bordeaux, Thiers made it clear to them that the peace preliminaries must be assented to at once, without even the honours of a Parliamentary debate, as the only condition on which Prussia would permit them to open the war against the Republic and Paris, its stronghold. The counter-revolution had, in fact, no time to lose. The Second Empire had more than doubled the national debt, and plunged all the large towns into heavy municipal debts. The war had fearfully swelled the liabilities, and mercilessly ravaged the resources of the nation. To complete the ruin, the Prussian Shylock was there with his bond for the keep of half a million of his soldiers on French soil, his indemnity of five milliards, and interest at 5 per cent on the unpaid instalments thereof. Who was to pay the bill? It was only by the violent overthrow of the Republic that the appropriators of wealth could hope to shift on the shoulders of its producers the cost of a war which they, the appropriators, had themselves originated. Thus, the immense ruin of France spurred on these patriotic representatives of land and capital, under the very eyes and patronage of the invader, to graft upon the foreign war a civil war—a slaveholders' rebellion.

There stood in the way of this conspiracy one great obstacle—Paris. To disarm Paris was the first condition of success. Paris was therefore summoned by Thiers to surrender its arms. Then Paris was exasperated by the frantic anti-republican demonstrations of the "Rural" Assembly and by Thiers' own equivocations about the legal status of the Republic; by the threat to decapitate and decapitalize Paris; the appointment of Orleanist ambassadors; Dufaure's laws on over-due commercial bills and house-rents, inflicting ruin on the commerce and industry of Paris; Pouyer-Quertier's tax of two centimes upon every copy of every imaginable publication; the sentences of death against Blanqui and Flourens; the suppression of the Republican journals; the transfer of the National Assembly to Versailles; the renewal of the state of siege declared by Palikao, and expired on the 4th of September; the appointment of Vinoy, the *Décembriseur*, as governor of Paris—of Valentin, the imperialist *gendarme*, as its prefect of police—and of Aurelle de Paladines, the Jesuit general, as the commander-in-chief of its National Guard.

And now we have to address a question to M. Thiers and the men of national defence, his under-strappers. It is known that, through the agency of M. Pouyer-Quertier, his finance minister, Thiers had contracted a loan of two milliards. Now, is it true, or not,—

1. That the business was so managed that a consideration of several hundred millions was secured for the private benefit of Thiers, Jules Favre, Ernest Picard, Pouyer-Quertier, and Jules Simon? and—

2. That no money was to be paid down until after the "pacification" of Paris?

At all events, there must have been something very pressing in the matter, for Thiers and Jules Favre, in the name of the majority of the Bordeaux Assembly, unblushingly solicited the immediate occupation of Paris by Prussian troops. Such, however, was not the game of Bismarck, as he sneeringly, and in public, told the admiring Frankfort philistines on his return to Germany.

II

Armed Paris was the only serious obstacle in the way of the counter-revolutionary conspiracy. Paris was, therefore, to be disarmed. On this point the Bordeaux Assembly was sincerity itself. If the roaring rant of its Rurals had not been audible enough, the surrender of Paris by Thiers to the tender mercies of the triumvirate of Vinoy the *Décembriseur,* Valentin the Bonapartist *gendarme,* and Aurelle de Paladines the Jesuit general, would have cut off even the last subterfuge of doubt. But while insultingly exhibiting the true purpose of the disarmament of Paris, the conspirators asked her to lay down her arms on a pretext which was the most glaring, the most barefaced of lies. The artillery of the Paris National Guard, said Thiers, belonged to the State, and to the State it must be returned. The fact was this: From the very day of the capitulation, by which Bismarck's prisoners had signed the surrender of France, but reserved to themselves a numerous body-guard for the express purpose of cowing Paris, Paris stood on the watch. The National Guard reorganized themselves and intrusted their supreme control to a Central Committee elected by their whole body, save some fragments of the old Bonapartist formations. On the eve of the entrance of the Prussians into

Paris, the Central Committee took measures for the removal to Montmartre, Belleville, and La Villette of the cannon and *mitrailleuses* treacherously abandoned by the *capitulards* in and about the very quarters the Prussians were to occupy. That artillery had been furnished by the subscriptions of the National Guard. As their private property, it was officially recognized in the capitulation of the 28th of January, and on that very title exempted from the general surrender, into the hands of the conqueror, of arms belonging to the government. And Thiers was so utterly destitute of even the flimsiest pretext for initiating the war against Paris, that he had to resort to the flagrant lie of the artillery of the National Guard being State property!

The seizure of her artillery was evidently but to serve as the preliminary to the general disarmament of Paris, and, therefore, of the Revolution of the 4th of September. But that Revolution had become the legal status of France. The republic, its work, was recognized by the conqueror in the terms of the capitulation. After the capitulation, it was acknowledged by all the foreign Powers, and in its name the National Assembly had been summoned. The Paris working men's revolution of the 4th of September was the only legal title of the National Assembly seated at Bordeaux, and of its executive. Without it, the National Assembly would at once have to give way to the *Corps Législatif*, elected in 1869 by universal suffrage under French, not under Prussian, rule, and forcibly dispersed by the arm of the Revolution. Thiers and his ticket-of-leave-men would have had to capitulate for safe conducts signed by Louis Bonaparte, to save them from a voyage to Cayenne.[25] The National Assembly, with its power of attorney to settle the terms of peace with Prussia, was but an incident of that Revolution, the true embodiment of which was still armed Paris, which had initiated it, undergone for it a five months' siege, with its horrors of famine, and made her prolonged resistance, despite Trochu's plan, the basis of an obstinate war of defence in the provinces. And Paris was now either to lay down her arms at the insulting behest of the rebellious slaveholders of Bordeaux, and acknowledge that her Revolution of the 4th of September meant nothing but a simple transfer of power from Louis Bonaparte to his Royal rivals; or she had to stand forward as the self-sacrificing champion of France, whose salvation from ruin, and whose regeneration were impossible, without the revolutionary overthrow of the political and social conditions that had engendered the Second Empire, and, under its fostering care, matured into utter rottenness. Paris, emaciated by a five months' famine, did not hesitate one moment. She heroically resolved to run all the hazards of a resistance against the French conspirators, even with Prussian cannon frowning upon her from her own forts. Still, in its abhorrence of the civil war into which Paris was to be goaded, the Central Committee continued to persist in a merely defensive attitude, despite the provocations of the Assembly, the usurpations of the Executive, and the menacing concentration of troops in and around Paris.

Thiers opened the civil war by sending Vinoy, at the head of a multitude of *sergents-de-ville* and some regiments of the line, upon a nocturnal expedition against Montmartre, there to seize, by surprise, the artillery of the National Guard. It is well known how this attempt broke down before the resistance of the National Guard and the fraternization of the line with the people. Aurelle de Paladines had printed beforehand his bulletin of victory, and Thiers held ready the placards announcing his measures of *coup d'état*. Now these had to be replaced by Thiers' appeals, imparting his magnanimous resolve to leave the National Guard in the possession of their arms, with which, he said, he felt sure they would rally round the Government against the rebels. Out of 300,000 National Guards only 300 responded to this summons to rally round little Thiers against themselves. The glorious working men's Revolution of the 18th March took undisputed sway of Paris. The Central Committee was its provisional government. Europe seemed, for a moment, to doubt whether its recent sensational performances of state and war had any reality in them, or whether they were the dreams of a long bygone past.

From the 18th of March to the entrance of the Versailles troops into Paris, the proletarian revolution remained so free from the acts of violence in which the revolutions, and still more the counter-revolutions, of the "better classes" abound, that no facts were left to its opponents to cry out about but the execution of Generals Lecomte and Clément Thomas, and the affair of the Place Vendôme.

One of the Bonapartist officers engaged in the nocturnal attempt against Montmartre, General Lecomte, had four times ordered the 81st line regiment to fire at an unarmed gathering in the Place Pigalle, and on their refusal fiercely insulted them. Instead of shooting women and children, his own men shot him. The inveterate habits acquired by the soldiery under the training of the enemies of the working class are, of course, not likely to change the very moment these soldiers change sides. The same men executed Clément Thomas.

"General" Clément Thomas, a malcontent exquartermaster-sergeant, had, in the latter times of Louis Philippe's reign, enlisted at the office of the Republican newspaper *Le National*,[26] there to serve in the double capacity of responsible man-of-straw (*gérant résponsable*) and of duelling bully to that very combative journal. After the revolution of February, the men of the *National* having got into power, they metamorphosed this old quartermaster-sergeant into a general on the eve of the butchery of June, of which he, like Jules Favre, was one of the sinister plotters, and became one of the most dastardly executioners. Then he and his generalship disappeared for a long time, to again rise to the surface on the 1st November, 1870. The day before the Government of Defence, caught at the Hôtel de Ville, had solemnly pledged their parole to Blanqui, Flourens, and other representatives of the working class, to abdicate their usurped power into the hands of a commune to be freely elected by Paris. Instead of keeping their word, they let loose on Paris the Bretons of Trochu, who now replaced the Corsicans of Bonaparte. General Tamisier alone, refusing to sully his name by such a breach of faith, resigned the commandership-in-chief of the National Guard, and in his place Clément Thomas for once became again a general. During the whole of his tenure of command, he made war, not upon the Prussians, but upon the Paris National Guard. He prevented their general armament, pitted the bourgeois battalions against the working men's battalions, weeded out the officers hostile to Trochu's "plan", and disbanded, under the stigma of cowardice, the very same proletarian battalions whose heroism has now astonished their most inveterate enemies. Clément Thomas felt quite proud of having reconquered his June pre-eminence as the personal enemy of the working class of Paris. Only a few days before the 18th of March, he laid before the War Minister, Le Flô, a plan of his own for "finishing off *la fine fleur* (the cream) of the Paris *canaille*." After Vinoy's rout, he must needs appear upon the scene of action in the quality of an amateur spy. The Central Committee and the Paris working men were as much responsible for the killing of Clément Thomas and Lecomte as the Princess of Wales was for the fate of the people crushed to death on the day of her entrance into London.

The massacre of unarmed citizens in the Place Vendôme is a myth which M. Thiers and the Rurals persistently ignored in the Assembly, intrusting its propagation exclusively to the servants' hall of European journalism. "The men of order," the reactionists of Paris, trembled at the victory of the 18th of March. To them it was the signal of popular retribution at last arriving. The ghosts of the victims assassinated at their hands from the days of June, 1848, down to the 22nd of January, 1871, arose before their faces. Their panic was their only punishment. Even the *sergents-de-ville*, instead of being disarmed and locked up, as ought to have been done, had the gates of Paris flung wide open for their safe retreat to Versailles. The men of order were left not only unharmed, but allowed to rally and quietly to seize more than one stronghold in the very centre of Paris. This indulgence of the Central Committee—this magnanimity of the armed working men—so strangely at variance with the habits of the "Party of Order," the latter misinterpreted as mere symptoms of conscious weakness. Hence their silly plan to try, under the cloak of an unarmed demonstration, what Vinoy had failed to perform with his cannon and *mitrailleuses*. On the 22nd of March a riotous mob of swells started from the quarters of luxury, all the *petits crevés* in their ranks, and at their head the notorious familiars of the Empire—the Heeckeren, Coetlogon, Henri de Pène, etc. Under the cowardly pretence of a pacific demonstration, this rabble, secretly armed with the weapons of the bravo,* fell into marching order, ill-treated and disarmed the detached patrols and sentries of the National Guards they met with on their progress, and, on debouching from the Rue de la Paix, with the cry of "Down with the Central Committee! Down with the assassins! The National Assembly for ever!" attempted to break through the line drawn up there, and thus to carry by a surprise the headquarters of the National Guard in the Place Vendôme. In reply to their pistol-shots, the regular *sommations* (the French equivalent of the English Riot Act) were made, and, proving ineffective, fire was commanded by the general of the National Guard. One volley dispersed into wild flight the silly coxcombs, who expected that the mere exhibition of their "respectability" would have the same effect upon the Revolution of Paris as Joshua's trumpets upon the walls of Jericho. The runaways left behind them two National Guards killed, nine severely wounded (among them a member of the Central Committee), and the whole scene of their exploit strewn with revolvers, daggers, and sword-canes, in evidence of the "unarmed" character of their "pacific" demonstration. When, on the 13th of June, 1849, the National Guard made a really pacific demonstration in protest against the felonious assault of French troops upon Rome, Changarnier, then general of the Party of Order, was acclaimed by the National Assembly, and especially by M. Thiers, as the saviour of society, for having launched his troops from all sides upon these unarmed men, to shoot and sabre them down, and to trample them under their horses' feet. Paris, then, was placed under a state of siege. Dufaure hurried through the Assembly new laws of repression. New arrests, new proscriptions—a new reign of terror set in. But the lower orders manage these things otherwise. The Central Committee of 1871 simply ignored the heroes of the "pacific demonstration"; so much so that only two days later they were enabled to muster under Admiral Saisset for that *armed* demonstration, crowned by the famous stampede to Versailles. In their

---

* Assassin.—*Ed.*

reluctance to continue the civil war opened by Thiers' burglarious attempt on Montmartre, the Central Committee made itself, this time, guilty of a decisive mistake in not at once marching upon Versailles, then completely helpless, and thus putting an end to the conspiracies of Thiers and his Rurals. Instead of this, the Party of Order was again allowed to try its strength at the ballot box, on the 26th of March, the day of the election of the Commune. Then, in the *mairies* of Paris, they exchanged bland words of conciliation with their too generous conquerors, muttering in their hearts solemn vows to exterminate them in due time.

Now look at the reverse of the medal. Thiers opened his second campaign against Paris in the beginning of April. The first batch of Parisian prisoners brought into Versailles was subjected to revolting atrocities, while Ernest Picard, with his hands in his trousers' pockets, strolled about jeering them, and while Mesdames Thiers and Favre, in the midst of their ladies of honour (?) applauded, from the balcony, the outrages of the Versailles mob. The captured soldiers of the line were massacred in cold blood; our brave friend, General Duval, the iron-founder, was shot without any form of trial. Galliffet, the kept man of his wife, so notorious for her shameless exhibitions at the orgies of the Second Empire, boasted in a proclamation of having commanded the murder of a small troop of National Guards, with their captain and lieutenant, surprised and disarmed by his Chasseurs. Vinoy, the runaway, was appointed by Thiers Grand Cross of the Legion of Honour, for his general order to shoot down every soldier of the line taken in the ranks of the Federals. Desmarêt, the gendarme, was decorated for the treacherous butcherlike chopping in pieces of the high-souled and chivalrous Flourens, who had saved the heads of the Government of Defence on the 31st of October, 1870. "The encouraging particulars" of his assassination were triumphantly expatiated upon by Thiers in the National Assembly. With the elated vanity of a parliamentary Tom Thumb, permitted to play the part of a Tamerlane, he denied the rebels against his littleness every right of civilized warfare, up to the right of neutrality for ambulances. Nothing more horrid than that monkey, allowed for a time to give full fling to his tigerish instincts, as foreseen by Voltaire. [27] (See note, p. 35.) *

After the decree of the Commune of the 7th April, ordering reprisals and declaring it to be its duty "to protect Paris against the cannibal exploits of the Versailles banditti, and to demand an eye for an eye, a tooth for a tooth," Thiers did not stop the barbarous treatment of prisoners, moreover insulting them in his bulletins as follows:—"Never have more degraded countenances of a degraded democracy met the afflicted gazes of honest men", —honest like Thiers himself and his ministerial ticket-of-leave-men. Still the shooting of prisoners was suspended for a time. Hardly, however, had Thiers and his Decembrist generals become aware that the Communal decree of reprisals was but an empty threat, that even their gendarme spies caught in Paris under the disguise of National Guards, that even *sergents-de-ville,* taken with incendiary shells upon them, were spared,—when the wholesale shooting of prisoners was resumed and carried on uninterruptedly to the end. Houses to which National Guards had fled were surrounded by gendarmes, inundated with petroleum (which here occurs for the first time in this war), and then set fire to, the charred corpses being afterwards brought out by the ambulance of the Press at the Ternes. Four National Guards having surrendered to a troop of mounted Chasseurs at Bell Epine, on the 25th of April, were afterwards shot down, one after another, by the captain, a worthy man of Galliffet's. One of his four victims, left for dead, Scheffer, crawled back to the Parisian outposts, and deposed to this fact before a commission of the Commune. When Tolain interpellated the War Minister upon the report of this commission, the Rurals drowned his voice and forbade Le Flô to answer. It would be an insult to their "glorious" army to speak of its deeds. The flippant tone in which Thiers' bulletins announced the bayoneting of the Federals surprised asleep at Moulin Saquet, and the wholesale fusillades at Clamart shocked the nerves even of the not oversensitive London *Times.* But it would be ludicrous today to attempt recounting the

---

* See Appendixes, p. 79 of this book.—*Ed.*

merely preliminary atrocities committed by the bombarders of Paris and the fomenters of a slaveholders' rebellion protected by foreign invasion. Amidst all these horrors, Thiers, forgetful of his parliamentary laments on the terrible responsibility weighing down his dwarfish shoulders, boasts in his bulletin that *l'Assemblée siège paisiblement* (the Assembly continues meeting in peace), and proves by his constant carousals, now with Decembrist generals, now with German princes, that his digestion is not troubled in the least, not even by the ghosts of Lecomte and Clément Thomas.

III

On the dawn of the 18th of March, Paris arose to the thunderburst of "Vive la Commune!" What is the Commune, that sphinx so tantalizing to the bourgeois mind?

"The proletarians of Paris," said the Central Committee in its manifesto of the 18th March, "amidst the failures and treasons of the ruling classes, have understood that the hour has struck for them to save the situation by taking into their own hands the direction of public affairs.... They have understood that it is their imperious duty and their absolute right to render themselves masters of their own destinies, by seizing upon the governmental power." But the working class cannot simply lay hold of the ready-made state machinery, and wield it for its own purposes.

The centralized State power, with its ubiquitous organs of standing army, police, bureaucracy, clergy, and judicature—organs wrought after the plan of a systematic and hierarchic division of labour,—originates from the days of absolute monarchy, serving nascent middle-class society as a mighty weapon in its struggles against feudalism. Still, its development remained clogged by all manner of mediaeval rubbish, seignorial rights, local privileges, municipal and guild monopolies and provincial constitutions. The gigantic broom of the French Revolution of the eighteenth century swept away all these relics of bygone times, thus clearing simultaneously the social soil of its last hindrances to the superstructure of the modern State edifice raised under the First Empire, itself the offspring of the coalition wars of old semi-feudal Europe against modern France. During the subsequent *régimes* the Government, placed under parliamentary control—that is, under the direct control of the propertied classes—became not only a hotbed of huge national debts and crushing taxes; with its irresistible allurements of place, pelf, and patronage, it became not only the bone of contention between the rival factions and adventurers of the ruling classes; but its political character changed simultaneously with the economic changes of society. At the same pace at which the progress of modern industry developed, widened, intensified the class antagonism between capital and labour, the State power assumed more and more the character of the national power of capital over labour, of a public force organized for social enslavement, of an engine of class despotism.* After every revolution marking a progressive phase in the class struggle, the purely repressive character of the State power stands out in bolder and bolder relief. The Revolution of 1830, resulting in the transfer of Government from the landlords to the capitalists, transferred it from the more remote to the more direct antagonists of the working men. The bourgeois Republicans, who, in the name of the Revolution of February, took the State power, used it for the June massacres, in order to convince the working class that "social" republic meant the republic ensuring their social subjection, and in order to convince the royalist bulk of the bourgeoisie and the landlord class that they might safely leave the cares and emoluments of Government to the bourgeois "Republicans." However, after their one heroic exploit of June, the bourgeois Republicans had, from the front, to fall back to the rear of the "Party of Order" —a combination formed by all the rival factions and parties of the appropriating class in their now openly declared antagonism to the producing classes. The proper form of their joint-stock Government was the *Parliamentary Republic*, with Louis Bonaparte for its President. Thiers was a *régime* of avowed class terrorism and deliberate insult

---

* In the German translation done by Engels in 1871 the latter part of this sentence is somewhat shortened, and reads: [assumed more and more] "the character of a public force for the oppression of labour, the character of a machine of class despotism."—*Ed.*

toward the "vile multitude." If the Parliamentary Republic, as M. Thiers said, "divided them (the different factions of the ruling class) least," it opened an abyss between that class and the whole body of society outside their spare ranks. The restraints by which their own divisions had under former *régimes* still checked the State power, were removed by their union; and in view of the threatening upheaval of the proletariat, they now used that State power mercilessly and ostentatiously as the national war-engine of capital against labour. In their uninterrupted crusade against the producing masses they were, however, bound not only to invest the executive with continually increased powers of repression, but at the same time to divest their own parliamentary stronghold—the National Assembly—one by one, of all its own means of defence against the Executive. The Executive, in the person of Louis Bonaparte, turned them out. The natural offspring of the "Party-of-Order" Republic was the Second Empire.

The Empire, with the *coup d'état* for its certificate of birth, universal suffrage for its sanction, and the sword for its sceptre, professed to rest upon the peasantry, the large mass of producers not directly involved in the struggle of capital and labour. It professed to save the working class by breaking down Parliamentarism, and, with it, the undisguised subserviency of Government to the propertied classes. It professed to save the propertied classes by upholding their economic supremacy over the working class; and, finally, it professed to unite all classes by reviving for all the chimera of national glory. In reality, it was the only form of government possible at a time when the bourgeoisie had already lost, and the working class had not yet acquired, the faculty of ruling the nation. It was acclaimed throughout the world as the saviour of society. Under its sway, bourgeois society, freed from political cares, attained a development unexpected even by itself. Its industry and commerce expanded to colossal dimensions; financial swindling celebrated cosmopolitan orgies; the misery of the masses was set off by a shameless display of gorgeous, meretricious and debased luxury. The State power, apparently soaring high above society, was at the same time itself the greatest scandal of that society and the very hotbed of all its corruptions. Its own rottenness and the rottenness of the society it had saved, were laid bare by the bayonet of Prussia, herself eagerly bent upon transferring the supreme seat of that *régime* from Paris to Berlin. Imperialism is, at the same time, the most prostitute and the ultimate form of the State power which nascent middle-class society had commenced to elaborate as a means of its own emancipation from feudalism, and which full-grown bourgeois society had finally transformed into a means for the enslavement of labour by capital.

The direct antithesis to the Empire was the Commune. The cry of "social republic," with which the revolution of February was ushered in by the Paris proletariat, did but express a vague aspiration after a Republic that was not only to supersede the monarchical form of class-rule, but class-rule itself. The Commune was the positive form of that Republic.

Paris, the central seat of the old governmental power, and, at the same time, the social stronghold of the French working class, had risen in arms against the attempt of Thiers and the Rurals to restore and perpetuate that old governmental power bequeathed to them by the Empire. Paris could resist only because, in consequence of the siege, it had got rid of the army, and replaced it by a National Guard, the bulk of which consisted of working men. This fact was now to be transformed into an institution. The first decree of the Commune, therefore, was the suppression of the standing army, and the substitution for it of the armed people.

The Commune was formed of the municipal councillors, chosen by universal suffrage in the various wards of the town, responsible and revocable at short terms. The majority of its members were naturally working men, or acknowledged representatives of the working class. The Commune was to be a working, not a parliamentary, body, executive and legislative at the same time. Instead of continuing to be the agent of the Central Government, the police was at once stripped of its political attributes, and turned into the responsible and at all times revocable agent of the Commune. So were the officials of all other branches of the Administration. From the members of the Commune downwards, the public service had to be done at *workmen's wages*. The vested interests and the representation allowances of the high dignitaries of State disappeared along with the high dignitaries themselves. Public functions ceased to be the private property of the tools of the Central Government. Not only municipal administration, but the whole initiative hitherto exercised by the State was laid into the hands of the Commune.

Having once got rid of the standing army and the police, the physical force elements of the old Government, the Commune was anxious to break the spiritual force of repression, the "parson-power," by the disestablishment and disendowment of all churches as proprietary bodies. The priests were sent back to the recesses of private life, there to feed upon the alms of the faithful in imitation of their predecessors, the Apostles. The whole of the educational institutions were opened to the people gratuitously, and at the same time cleared of all interference of Church and State. Thus, not only was education made accessible to all, but science itself freed from the fetters which class prejudice and governmental force had imposed upon it.

The judicial functionaries were to be divested of that sham independence which had but served to mask their abject subserviency to all succeeding governments to which, in turn, they had taken, and broken, the oaths of allegiance. Like the rest of public servants, magistrates and judges were to be elective, responsible, and revocable.

The Paris Commune was, of course, to serve as a model to all the great industrial centres of France. The communal *régime* once established in Paris and the secondary centres, the old centralized Government would in the provinces, too, have to give way to the self-government of the producers. In a rough sketch of national organization which the Commune had no time to develop, it states clearly that the Commune was to be the political form of even the smallest country hamlet, and that in the rural districts the standing army was to be replaced by a national militia, with an extremely short term of service. The rural communes of every district were to administer their common affairs by an assembly of delegates in the central town, and these district assemblies were again to send deputies to the National Delegation in Paris, each delegate to be at any time revocable and bound by the *mandat impératif* (formal instructions) of his constituents. The few but important functions which still would remain for a central government were not to be suppressed, as has been intentionally mis-stated, but were to be discharged by Communal, and therefore strictly responsible, agents. The unity of the nation was not to be broken, but, on the contrary, to be organized by the Communal Constitution, and to become a reality by the destruction of the State power which claimed to be the embodiment of that unity independent of, and superior to, the nation itself, from which it was but a parasitic excrescence. While the merely repressive organs of the old governmental power were to be amputated, its legitimate functions were to be wrested from an authority usurping pre-eminence over society itself, and restored to the responsible agents of society. Instead of deciding once in three or six years which member of the ruling class was to misrepresent the people in Parliament, universal suffrage was to serve the people, constituted in Communes, as individual suffrage serves every other employer in the search for the workmen and managers in his business. And it is well known that companies, like individuals, in matters of real business generally know how to put the right man in the right place, and, if they for once make a mistake, to redress it promptly. On the other hand, nothing could be more foreign to the spirit of the Commune than to supersede universal suffrage by hierarchic investiture.[28]

It is generally the fate of completely new historical creations to be mistaken for the counterpart of older and even defunct forms of social life, to which they may bear a certain likeness. Thus, this new Commune, which breaks the modern State power, has been mistaken for a reproduction of the mediaeval Communes, which first preceded, and afterwards became the substratum of, that very State power. The Communal Constitution has been mistaken for an attempt to break up into a federation of small States, as dreamt of by Montesquieu and the Girondins, that unity of great nations which, if originally brought about by political force, has now become a powerful coefficient of social production. The antagonism of the

Commune against the State power has been mistaken for an exaggerated form of the ancient struggle against over-centralization. Peculiar historical circumstances may have prevented the classical development, as in France, of the bourgeois form of government, and may have allowed, as in England, to complete the great central State organs by corrupt vestries, jobbing councillors, and ferocious poor-law guardians in the towns, and virtually hereditary magistrates in the counties. The Communal Constitution would have restored to the social body all the forces hitherto absorbed by the State parasite feeding upon, and clogging the free movement of, society. By this one act it would have initiated the regeneration of France. The provincial French middle class saw in the Commune an attempt to restore the sway their order had held over the country under Louis Philippe, and which, under Louis Napoleon, was supplanted by the pretended rule of the country over the towns. In reality, the Communal Constitution brought the rural producers under the intellectual lead of the central towns of their districts, and these secured to them, in the working men, the natural trustees of their interests. The very existence of the Commune involved, as a matter of course, local municipal liberty, but no longer as a check upon the, now superseded, State power. It could only enter into the head of a Bismarck, who, when not engaged on his intrigues of blood and iron, always likes to resume his old trade, so befitting his mental calibre, of contributor to *Kladderadatsch* (the Berlin Punch),[29] it could only enter into such a head, to ascribe to the Paris Commune aspirations after that caricature of the old French municipal organization of 1791, the Prussian municipal constitution, which degrades the town governments to mere secondary wheels in the police-machinery of the Prussian State.

The Commune made that catchword of bourgeois revolutions, cheap government, a reality, by destroying the two greatest sources of expenditure—the standing army and State functionarism. Its very existence presupposed the non-existence of monarchy, which, in Europe at least, is the normal incumbrance and indispensable cloak of class-rule. It supplied the Republic with the basis of really democratic institutions. But neither cheap Government nor the "true Republic" was its ultimate aim; they were its mere concomitants.

The multiplicity of interpretations to which the Commune has been subjected, and the multiplicity of interests which construed it in their favour, show that it was a thoroughly expansive political form, while all previous forms of government had been emphatically repressive. Its true secret was this. It was essentially a working-class government, the produce of the struggle of the producing against the appropriating class, the political form at last discovered under which to work out the economic emancipation of labour.

Except on this last condition, the Communal Constitution would have been an impossibility and a delusion. The political rule of the producer cannot coexist with the perpetuation of his social slavery. The Commune was therefore to serve as a lever for uprooting the economical foundations upon which rests the existence of classes, and therefore of class-rule. With labour emancipated, every man becomes a working man, and productive labour ceases to be a class attribute.

It is a strange fact. In spite of all the tall talk and all the immense literature, for the last sixty years, about Emancipation of Labour, no sooner do the working men anywhere take the subject into their own hands with a will, than uprises at once all the apologetic phraseology of the mouthpieces of present society with its two poles of Capital and Wages Slavery (the landlord now is but the sleeping partner of the capitalist), as if capitalist society was still in its purest state of virgin innocence, with its antagonisms still undeveloped, with its delusions still unexploded, with its prostitute realities not yet laid bare. The Commune, they exclaim, intends to abolish property, the basis of all civilization! Yes, gentlemen, the Commune intended to abolish that class-property which makes the labour of the many the wealth of the few. It aimed at the expropriation of the expropriators. It wanted to make individual property a truth by transforming the means of production, land and capital, now chiefly the means of enslaving and exploiting labour, into mere instruments of free and associated labour.— But this is Communism, "impossible" Communism! Why, those members of the ruling classes who are intelligent enough to perceive the impossibility of continuing the present system—and they are many—have become the obtrusive and full-mouthed apostles of co-operative production. If co-operative production is not to remain a sham and a snare; if it is to supersede the Capitalist system; if united co-operative societies are to regulate national production upon a common plan, thus taking it under their own control, and putting an end to the constant anarchy and periodical convulsions which are the fatality of Capitalist production—what else, gentlemen, would it be but Communism, "possible" Communism?

The working class did not expect miracles from the Commune. They have no ready-made utopias to introduce *par décret du peuple*.* They know that in order to work out their own emancipation, and along with it that higher form to which present society is irresistibly tending by its own economic agencies, they will have to pass through long struggles, through a series of historic processes, transforming circumstances and men. They have no ideals to realize, but to set free the elements of the new society with which old collapsing bourgeois society itself is pregnant. In the full consciousness of their historic mission, and with the heroic resolve to act up to it, the working class can afford to smile at the coarse invective of the gentlemen's gentlemen with the pen and inkhorn, and at the didactic patronage of well-wishing bourgeois-doctrinaires, pouring forth their ignorant platitudes and sectarian crotchets in the oracular tone of scientific infallibility.

When the Paris Commune took the management of the revolution in its own hands; when plain working men for the first time dared to infringe upon the Governmental privilege of their "natural superiors," and, under circumstances of unexampled difficulty, performed their work modestly, conscientiously, and efficiently,—performed it at salaries the highest of which barely amounted to one-fifth of what, according to high scientific authority,** is the minimum required for a secretary to a certain metropolitan school board,—the old world writhed in convulsions of

---

* By decree of the people.—*Ed.*
** Professor Huxley. *(Note to the German edition of 1871.)*

rage at the sight of the Red Flag, the symbol of the Republic of Labour, floating over the Hôtel de Ville.

And yet, this was the first revolution in which the working class was openly acknowledged as the only class capable of social initiative, even by the great bulk of the Paris middle class—shopkeepers, tradesmen, merchants—the wealthy capitalists alone excepted. The Commune had saved them by a sagacious settlement of that ever-recurring cause of dispute among the middle classes themselves—the debtor and creditor accounts.* The same portion of the middle class, after they had assisted in putting down the working men's insurrection of June, 1848, had been at once unceremoniously sacrificed to their creditors by the then Constituent Assembly. But this was not their only motive for now rallying round the working class. They felt that there was but one alternative—the Commune, or the Empire—under whatever name it might reappear. The Empire had ruined them economically by the havoc it made of public wealth, by the wholesale financial swindling it fostered, by the props it lent to the artificially accelerated centralization of capital, and the concomitant expropriation of their own ranks. It had suppressed them politically, it had shocked them morally by its orgies, it had insulted their Voltairianism by handing over the education of their children to the *frères Ignorantins,* it had revolted their national feeling as Frenchmen by precipitating them headlong into a war which left only one equivalent for the ruins it made—the disappearance of the Empire. In fact, after the exodus from Paris of the high Bonapartist and capitalist *bohême,* the true middle-class Party of Order came out in the shape of the "Union Républicaine," enrolling themselves under the colours of the Commune and defending it against the willful misconstruction of Thiers. Whether the gratitude of this great body of the middle class will stand the present severe trial, time must show.

The Commune was perfectly right in telling the peasants that "its victory was their only hope." Of all the lies hatched at Versailles and re-echoed by the glorious European penny-a-liner, one of the most tremendous was that the

---

* On April 18, the Commune promulgated a decree postponing payments on debt obligations for three years.—*Ed.*

Rurals represented the French peasantry. Think only of the love of the French peasant for the men to whom, after 1815, he had to pay the milliard of indemnity. In the eyes of the French peasant, the very existence of a great landed proprietor is in itself an encroachment on his conquests of 1789. The bourgeois, in 1848, had burdened his plot of land with the additional tax of forty-five cents in the franc; but then he did so in the name of the revolution; while now he had fomented a civil war against the revolution, to shift on to the peasant's shoulders the chief load of the five milliards of indemnity to be paid to the Prussians. The Commune, on the other hand, in one of its first proclamations, declared that the true originators of the war would be made to pay its cost. The Commune would have delivered the peasant of the blood tax,—would have given him a cheap government,—transformed his present bloodsuckers, the notary, advocate, executor, and other judicial vampires, into salaried communal agents, elected by, and responsible to, himself. It would have freed him of the tyranny of the *garde champêtre*,* the gendarme, and the prefect; would have put enlightenment by the schoolmaster in the place of stultification by the priest. And the French peasant is, above all, a man of reckoning. He would find it extremely reasonable that the pay of the priest, instead of being extorted by the taxgatherer, should only depend upon the spontaneous action of the parishioners' religious instincts. Such were the great immediate boons which the rule of the Commune—and that rule alone—held out to the French peasantry. It is, therefore, quite superfluous here to expatiate upon the more complicated but vital problems which the Commune alone was able, and at the same time compelled, to solve in favour of the peasant, *viz.*, the hypothecary debt, lying like an incubus upon his parcel of soil, the *prolétariat foncier* (the rural proletariat), daily growing upon it, and his expropriation from it enforced, at a more and more rapid rate, by the very development of modern agriculture and the competition of capitalist farming.

The French peasant had elected Louis Bonaparte President of the Republic; but the Party of Order created

---

* Village policeman.—*Ed*.

the Empire. What the French peasant really wants he commenced to show in 1849 and 1850, by opposing his *maire* to the Government's prefect, his schoolmaster to the Government's priest, and himself to the Government's gendarme. All the laws made by the Party of Order in January and February, 1850, were avowed measures of repression against the peasant. The peasant was a Bonapartist, because the great Revolution, with all its benefits to him, was, in his eyes, personified in Napoleon. This delusion, rapidly breaking down under the Second Empire (and in its very nature hostile to the Rurals), this prejudice of the past, how could it have withstood the appeal of the Commune to the living interests and urgent wants of the peasantry?

The Rurals—this was, in fact, their chief apprehension —knew that three months' free communication of Communal Paris with the provinces would bring about a general rising of the peasants, and hence their anxiety to establish a police blockade around Paris, so as to stop the spread of the rinderpest.

If the Commune was thus the true representative of all the healthy elements of French society, and therefore the truly national Government, it was, at the same time, as a working men's Government, as the bold champion of the emancipation of labour, emphatically international. Within sight of the Prussian army, that had annexed to Germany two French provinces, the Commune annexed to France the working people all over the world.

The Second Empire had been the jubilee of cosmopolitan black-leggism, the rakes of all countries rushing in at its call for a share in its orgies and in the plunder of the French people. Even at this moment the right hand of Thiers is Ganesco, the foul Wallachian, and his left hand is Markovsky, the Russian spy. The Commune admitted all foreigners to the honour of dying for an immortal cause. Between the foreign war lost by their treason, and the civil war fomented by their conspiracy with the foreign invader, the bourgeoisie had found the time to display their patriotism by organizing police-hunts upon the Germans in France. The Commune made a German working man its Minister of Labour. Thiers, the bourgeoisie, the Second Empire, had continually deluded Poland by loud professions of sympathy, while in reality betraying her to, and doing the dirty work of, Russia. The Commune honoured the heroic sons of Poland by placing them at the head of the defenders of Paris. And, to broadly mark the new era of history it was conscious of initiating, under the eyes of the conquering Prussians, on the one side, and of the Bonapartist army, led by Bonapartist generals, on the other, the Commune pulled down that colossal symbol of martial glory, the Vendôme column. 30

The great social measure of the Commune was its own working existence. Its special measures could but betoken the tendency of a government of the people by the people. Such were the abolition of the nightwork of journeymen bakers; the prohibition, under penalty, of the employers' practice to reduce wages by levying fines upon their workpeople under manifold pretexts,—a process in which the employer combines in his own person the parts of legislator, judge, and executor, and filches the money to boot. Another measure of this class was the surrender, to associations of workmen under reserve of compensation, of all closed workshops and factories, no matter whether the respective capitalists had absconded or preferred to strike work.

The financial measures of the Commune, remarkable for their sagacity and moderation, could only be such as were compatible with the state of a besieged town. Considering the colossal robberies committed upon the city of Paris by the great financial companies and contractors, under the protection of Haussmann,* the Commune would have had an incomparably better title to confiscate their property than Louis Napoleon had against the Orleans family. The Hohenzollern and the English oligarchs, who both have derived a good deal of their estates from Church plunder, were, of course, greatly shocked at the Commune clearing but 8,000 francs out of secularization. While the Versailles Government, as soon as it had recovered some spirit and strength, used the most violent means against the Com-

---

* During the Second Empire, Baron Haussmann was Prefect of the Department of the Seine, that is, of the City of Paris. He introduced a number of changes in the layout of the city for the purpose of facilitating the crushing of workers' insurrections. [*Note to the Russian translation edited by* V. I. Lenin.]

mune; while it put down the free expression of opinion all over France, even to the forbidding of meetings of delegates from the large towns; while it subjected Versailles and the rest of France to an espionage far surpassing that of the Second Empire; while it burned by its gendarme inquisitors all papers printed at Paris, and sifted all correspondence from and to Paris; while in the National Assembly the most timid attempts to put in a word for Paris were howled down in a manner unknown even to the *Chambre introuvable* of 1816; with the savage warfare of Versailles outside, and its attempts at corruption and conspiracy inside Paris—would the Commune not have shamefully betrayed its trust by affecting to keep up all the decencies and appearances of liberalism as in a time of profound peace? Had the Government of the Commune been akin to that of M. Thiers, there would have been no more occasion to suppress Party-of-Order papers at Paris than there was to suppress Communal papers at Versailles.

It was irritating indeed to the Rurals that at the very same time they declared the return to the church to be the only means of salvation for France, the infidel Commune unearthed the peculiar mysteries of the Picpus nunnery, and of the Church of Saint Laurent. It was a satire upon M. Thiers that, while he showered grand crosses upon the Bonapartist generals in acknowledgement of their mastery in losing battles, signing capitulations, and turning cigarettes at Wilhelmshöhe, the Commune dismissed and arrested its generals whenever they were suspected of neglecting their duties. The expulsion from, and arrest by, the Commune of one of its members who had slipped in under a false name, and had undergone at Lyons six days' imprisonment for simple bankruptcy, was it not a deliberate insult hurled at the forger, Jules Favre, then still the Foreign Minister of France, still selling France to Bismarck, and still dictating his orders to that paragon Government of Belgium? But indeed the Commune did not pretend to infallibility, the invariable attribute of all governments of the old stamp. It published its doings and sayings, it initiated the public into all its shortcomings.

In every revolution there intrude, at the side of its true agents, men of a different stamp; some of them survivors of and devotees to past revolutions, without insight into the present movement, but preserving popular influence by their known honesty and courage, or by the sheer force of tradition; others mere bawlers, who, by dint of repeating year after year the same set of stereotyped declamations against the Government of the day, have sneaked into the reputation of revolutionists of the first water. After the 18th of March, some such men did also turn up, and in some cases contrived to play pre-eminent parts. As far as their power went, they hampered the real action of the working class, exactly as men of that sort have hampered the full development of every previous revolution. They are an unavoidable evil: with time they are shaken off; but time was not allowed to the Commune.

Wonderful, indeed, was the change the Commune had wrought in Paris! No longer any trace of the meretricious Paris of the Second Empire. No longer was Paris the rendezvous of British landlords, Irish absentees, [31] American ex-slaveholders and shoddy men,* Russian ex-serfowners, and Wallachian boyards. No more corpses at the morgue, no nocturnal burglaries, scarcely any robberies; in fact, for the first time since the days of February, 1848, the streets of Paris were safe, and that without any police of any kind. "We," said a member of the Commune, "hear no longer of assassination, theft and personal assault; it seems indeed as if the police had dragged along with it to Versailles all its Conservative friends." The *cocottes* had refound the scent of their protectors—the absconding men of family, religion, and, above all, of property. In their stead, the real women of Paris showed again at the surface—heroic, noble, and devoted, like the women of antiquity. Working, thinking, fighting, bleeding Paris—almost forgetful, in its incubation of a new society, of the cannibals at its gates—radiant in the enthusiasm of its historic initiative!

Opposed to this new world at Paris, behold the old world at Versailles—that assembly of the ghouls of all defunct *régimes*, Legitimists and Orleanists, eager to feed upon the carcass of the nation,—with a tail of antediluvian Republicans, sanctioning, by their presence in the Assembly, the slaveholders' rebellion, relying for the maintenance of

---

* *Shoddy men*—upstarts.—*Ed.*

their Parliamentary Republic upon the vanity of the senile mountebank at its head, and caricaturing 1789 by holding their ghastly meetings in the *Jeu de Paume*.* There it was, this Assembly, the representative of everything dead in France, propped up to the semblance of life by nothing but the swords of the generals of Louis Bonaparte. Paris all truth, Versailles all lie; and that lie he vented through the mouth of Thiers.

Thiers tells a deputation of the mayors of the Seine-et-Oise,—"You may rely upon my word, which I have *never* broken!" He tells the Assembly itself that "it was the most freely elected and most Liberal Assembly France ever possessed"; he tells his motley soldiery that it was "the admiration of the world, and the finest army France ever possessed"; he tells the provinces that the bombardment of Paris by him was a myth: "If some cannon-shots have been fired, it is not the deed of the army of Versailles, but of some insurgents trying to make believe that they are fighting, while they dare not show their faces." He again tells the provinces that "the artillery of Versailles does not bombard Paris, but only cannonades it." He tells the Archbishop of Paris that the pretended executions and reprisals (!) attributed to the Versailles troops were all moonshine. He tells Paris that he was only anxious "to free it from the hideous tyrants who oppress it," and that, in fact, the Paris of the Commune was "but a handful of criminals."

The Paris of M. Thiers was not the real Paris of the "vile multitude," but a phantom Paris, the Paris of the *francs-fileurs*, the Paris of the Boulevards, male and female—the rich, the capitalist, the gilded, the idle Paris, now thronging with its lackeys, its blacklegs its literary *bohême*, and its *cocottes* at Versailles, Saint-Denis, Rueil, and Saint-Germain; considering the civil war but an agreeable diversion, eyeing the battle going on through telescopes, counting the rounds of cannon, and swearing by their own honour and that of their prostitutes, that the performance was far better got up than it used to be at the Porte St.

---

* *Jeu de Paume*—the tennis court where the National Assembly of 1789 adopted its famous decision. [*Note to the German edition of 1871.*]

Martin. The men who fell were really dead; the cries of the wounded were cries in good earnest; and, besides, the whole thing was so intensely historical.

This is the Paris of M. Thiers, as the emigration of Coblenz [32] was the France of M. de Calonne.

IV

The first attempt of the slaveholders' conspiracy to put down Paris by getting the Prussians to occupy it, was frustrated by Bismarck's refusal. The second attempt, that of the 18th of March, ended in the rout of the army and the flight to Versailles of the Government, which ordered the whole administration to break up and follow in its track. By the semblance of peace-negotiations with Paris, Thiers found the time to prepare for war against it. But where to find an army? The remnants of the line regiments were weak in number and unsafe in character. His urgent appeal to the provinces to succour Versailles, by their National Guards and volunteers, met with a flat refusal. Brittany alone furnished a handful of *Chouans* [33] fighting under a white flag, every one of them wearing on his breast the heart of Jesus in white cloth, and shouting *"Vive le Roi!"* (Long live the King!) Thiers was, therefore, compelled to collect, in hot haste a motley crew, composed of sailors, marines, Pontifical Zouaves, [34] Valentin's gendarmes, and Pietri's *sergents-de-ville* and *mouchards*. This army, however, would have been ridiculously ineffective without the instalments of imperialist war-prisoners, which Bismarck granted in numbers just sufficient to keep the civil war going, and keep the Versailles Government in abject dependence on Prussia. During the war itself, the Versailles police had to look after the Versailles army, while the gendarmes had to drag it on by exposing themselves at all posts of danger. The forts which fell were not taken, but bought. The heroism of the Federals convinced Thiers that the resistance of Paris was not to be broken by his own strategic genius and the bayonets at his disposal.

Meanwhile, his relations with the provinces became more and more difficult. Not one single address of approval came in to gladden Thiers and his Rurals. Quite the contrary. Deputations and addresses demanding, in a tone anything but respectful, conciliation with Paris on the basis of the unequivocal recognition of the Republic, the acknowledgement of the Communal liberties, and the dissolution of the National Assembly, whose mandate was extinct, poured in from all sides, and in such numbers that Dufaure, Thiers' Minister of Justice, in his circular of April 23 to the public prosecutors, commanded them to treat "the cry of conciliation" as a crime! In regard, however, of the hopeless prospect held out by his campaign, Thiers resolved to shift his tactics by ordering, all over the country, municipal elections to take place on the 30th of April, on the basis of the new municipal law dictated by himself to the National Assembly. What with the intrigues of his prefects, what with police intimidation, he felt quite sanguine of imparting, by the verdict of the provinces, to the National Assembly that moral power it had never possessed, and of getting at last from the provinces the physical force required for the conquest of Paris.

His banditti-warfare against Paris, exalted in his own bulletins, and the attempts of his ministers at the establishment, throughout France, of a reign of terror, Thiers was from the beginning anxious to accompany with a little by-play of conciliation, which had to serve more than one purpose. It was to dupe the provinces, to inveigle the middle-class element in Paris, and, above all, to afford the professed Republicans in the National Assembly the opportunity of hiding their treason against Paris behind their faith in Thiers. On the 21st of March, when still without an army, he had declared to the Assembly: "Come what may, I will not send an army to Paris." On the 27th March he rose again: "I have found the Republic an accomplished fact, and I am firmly resolved to maintain it." In reality, he put down the revolution at Lyons and Marseilles* in the name of the Republic, while the roars of his Rurals drowned the very mention of its name at Versailles. After this exploit, he toned down the "accomplished fact" into an hypothetical fact. The Orleans princes, whom he had cautiously warned off Bordeaux, were now, in flagrant

---

* A few days after March 18, 1871, revolutionary outbreaks occurred in Lyons and Marseilles aimed at the proclamation of Communes. The movement was crushed by the Thiers government.—*Ed.*

breach of the law, permitted to intrigue at Dreux. The concessions held out by Thiers in his interminable interviews with the delegates from Paris and the provinces, although constantly varied in tone and colour, according to time and circumstances, did in fact never come to more than the prospective restriction of revenge to the "handful of criminals implicated in the murder of Lecomte and Clément Thomas," on the well-understood premise that Paris and France were unreservedly to accept M. Thiers himself as the best of possible Republics, as he, in 1830, had done with Louis Philippe. Even these concessions he not only took care to render doubtful by the official comments put upon them in the Assembly through his Ministers. He had his Dufaure to act. Dufaure, this old Orleanist lawyer, had always been the justiciary of the state of siege, as now in 1871, under Thiers so in 1839 under Louis Philippe, and in 1849 under Louis Bonaparte's presidency. While out of office he made a fortune by pleading for the Paris capitalists, and made political capital by pleading against the laws he had himself originated. He now hurried through the National Assembly not only a set of repressive laws which were, after the fall of Paris, to extirpate the last remnants of Republican liberty in France; he foreshadowed the fate of Paris by abridging the, for him, too slow procedure of courts-martial, and by a new-fangled, Draconic code of deportation. The Revolution of 1848, abolishing the penalty of death for political crimes, has replaced it by deportation. Louis Bonaparte did not dare, at least not in theory, to re-establish the *régime* of the guillotine. The Rural Assembly, not yet bold enough even to hint that the Parisians were not rebels, but assassins, had therefore to confine its prospective vengeance against Paris to Dufaure's new code of deportation. Under all these circumstances Thiers himself could not have gone on with his comedy of conciliation, had it not, as he intended it to do, drawn forth shrieks of rage from the Rurals, whose ruminating mind did neither understand the play, nor its necessities of hypocrisy, tergiversation, and procrastination.

In sight of the impending municipal elections of the 30th April, Thiers enacted one of his great conciliation scenes on the 27th April. Amidst a flood of sentimental rhetoric, he exclaimed from the tribune of the Assembly: "There exists no conspiracy against the Republic but that of Paris, which compels us to shed French blood. I repeat it again and again. Let those impious arms fall from the hands which hold them, and chastisement will be arrested at once by an act of peace excluding only the small number of criminals." To the violent interruption of the Rurals he replied: "Gentlemen, tell me, I implore you, am I wrong? Do you really regret that I could have stated the truth that the criminals are only a handful? Is it not fortunate in the midst of our misfortunes that those who have been capable of shedding the blood of Clément Thomas and General Lecomte are but rare exceptions?"

France, however, turned a deaf ear to what Thiers flattered himself to be a parliamentary siren's song. Out of 700,000 municipal councillors returned by the 35,000 communes still left to France, the united Legitimists, Orleanists and Bonapartists did not carry 8,000. The supplementary elections which followed were still more decidedly hostile. Thus, instead of getting from the provinces the badly-needed physical force, the National Assembly lost even its last claim to moral force, that of being the expression of the universal suffrage of the country. To complete the discomfiture, the newly-chosen municipal councils of all the cities of France openly threatened the usurping Assembly at Versailles with a counter Assembly at Bordeaux.

Then the long-expected moment of decisive action had at last come for Bismarck. He peremptorily summoned Thiers to send to Frankfort plenipotentiaries for the definitive settlement of peace. In humble obedience to the call of his master, Thiers hastened to despatch his trusty Jules Favre, backed by Pouyer-Quertier. Pouyer-Quertier, an "eminent" Rouen cotton-spinner, a fervent and even servile partisan of the Second Empire, had never found any fault with it save its commercial treaty with England, prejudicial to his own shop-interest. Hardly installed at Bordeaux as Thiers' Minister of Finance, he denounced that "unholy" treaty, hinted at its near abrogation, and had even the effrontery to try, although in vain (having counted without Bismarck), the immediate enforcement of the old protective duties against Alsace, where, he said, no previous international treaties stood in the way. This man, who considered counter-revolution as a means to put down wages at Rouen, and the surrender of French provinces as a means to bring up the price of his wares in France, was he not *the one* predestined to be picked out by Thiers as the helpmate of Jules Favre in his last and crowning treason?

On the arrival at Frankfort of this exquisite pair of plenipotentiaries, bully Bismarck at once met them with the imperious alternative: Either the restoration of the Empire, or the unconditional acceptance of my own peace terms! These terms included a shortening of the intervals in which the war indemnity was to be paid and the continued occupation of the Paris forts by Prussian troops until Bismarck should feel satisfied with the state of things in France; Prussia thus being recognized as the supreme arbiter in internal French politics! In return for this he offered to let loose, for the extermination of Paris, the captive Bonapartist army, and to lend them the direct assistance of Emperor William's troops. He pledged his good faith by making payment of the first instalment of the indemnity dependent on the "pacification" of Paris. Such a bait was, of course, eagerly swallowed by Thiers and his plenipotentiaries. They signed the treaty of peace on the 10th of May, and had it endorsed by the Versailles Assembly on the 18th.

In the interval between the conclusion of peace and the arrival of the Bonapartist prisoners, Thiers felt the more bound to resume his comedy of conciliation, as his Republican tools stood in sore need of a pretext for blinking their eyes at the preparations for the carnage of Paris. As late as the 8th of May he replied to a deputation of middle-class conciliators: "Whenever the insurgents will make up their minds for capitulation, the gates of Paris shall be flung wide open during a week for all except the murderers of Generals Clément Thomas and Lecomte."

A few days afterwards, when violently interpellated on these promises by the Rurals, he refused to enter into any explanations; not, however, without giving them this significant hint: "I tell you there are impatient men amongst you, men who are in too great a hurry. They must wait another eight days; at the end of these eight days there will be no more danger, and the task will be proportionate to their courage and to their capacities." As soon as MacMahon was able to assure him that he could shortly enter Paris, Thiers declared to the Assembly that "he would enter Paris with the *law* in his hands, and demand a full expiation from the wretches who had sacrificed the lives of soldiers and destroyed public monuments." As the moment of decision drew near he said—to the Assembly, "I shall be pitiless!"—to Paris, that it was doomed; and to his Bonapartist banditti, that they had State licence to wreak vengeance upon Paris to their hearts' content. At last, when treachery had opened the gates of Paris to General Douay, on the 21st of May, Thiers, on the 22nd, revealed to the Rurals the "goal" of his conciliation comedy, which they had so obstinately persisted in not understanding. "I told you a few days ago that we were approaching *our goal*; today I come to tell you *the goal* is reached. The victory of order, justice and civilization is at last won!"

So it was. The civilization and justice of bourgeois order comes out in its lurid light whenever the slaves and drudges of that order rise against their masters. Then this civilization and justice stand forth as undisguised savagery and lawless revenge. Each new crisis in the class struggle between the appropriator and the producer brings out this fact more glaringly. Even the atrocities of the bourgeoisie in June, 1848, vanish before the ineffable infamy of 1871. The self-sacrificing heroism with which the population of Paris—men, women and children—fought for eight days after the entrance of the Versaillese, reflects as much the grandeur of their cause, as the infernal deeds of the soldiery reflect the innate spirit of that civilization of which they are the mercenary vindicators. A glorious civilization, indeed, the great problem of which is how to get rid of the heaps of corpses it made after the battle was over!

To find a parallel for the conduct of Thiers and his bloodhounds we must go back to the times of Sulla and the two Triumvirates of Rome. The same wholesale slaughter in cold blood; the same disregard, in massacre, of age and sex; the same system of torturing prisoners; the same proscriptions, but this time of a whole class; the same savage hunt after concealed leaders, lest one might escape; the same denunciations of political and private enemies; the same indifference for the butchery of entire strangers to the feud. There is but this difference, that the Romans had no *mitrailleuses* for the despatch, in the lump, of the proscribed, and that they had not "the law in their hands," nor on their lips the cry of "civilization."

And after those horrors, look upon the other, still more hideous, face of that bourgeois civilization as described by its own press!

"With stray shots," writes the Paris correspondent of a London Tory paper, "still ringing in the distance, and untended wounded wretches dying amid the tombstones of Père la Chaise—with 6,000 terror-stricken insurgents wandering in an agony of despair in the labyrinth of the catacombs, and wretches hurried through the streets to be shot down in scores by the *mitrailleuse*—it is revolting to see the *cafés* filled with the votaries of absinthe, billiards, and dominoes; female profligacy perambulating the boulevards, and the sound of revelry disturbing the night from the *cabinets particuliers* of fashionable restaurants." M. Edouard Hervé writes in the *Journal de Paris*, a Versaillist journal suppressed by the Commune: "The way in which the population of Paris (!) manifested its satisfaction yesterday was rather more than frivolous, and we fear it will grow worse as time progresses. Paris has now a *fête* day appearance, which is sadly out of place; and, unless we are to be called the *Parisiens de la décadence*,* this sort of thing must come to an end." And then he quotes the passage from Tacitus: "Yet, on the morrow of that horrible struggle, even before it was completely over, Rome—degraded and corrupt—began once more to wallow in the voluptuous slough which was destroying its body and polluting its soul—*alibi proelia et vulnera, alibi balnea popinaeque* (here fights and wounds, there baths and restaurants)." M. Hervé only forgets to say that the "population of Paris" he speaks of is but the population of the Paris of M. Thiers—the *francs-fileurs* returning in throngs from Versailles, Saint-Denis, Rueil and Saint-Germain—*the* Paris of the "Decline."

In all its bloody triumphs over the self-sacrificing cham-

---

* Parisians of the Decline.—*Ed*.

pions of a new and better society, that nefarious civilization, based upon the enslavement of labour, drowns the moans of its victims in a hue-and-cry of calumny, reverberated by a world-wide echo. The serene working men's Paris of the Commune is suddenly changed into a pandemonium by the bloodhounds of "order." And what does this tremendous change prove to the bourgeois mind of all countries? Why, that the Commune has conspired against civilization! The Paris people die enthusiastically for the Commune in numbers unequalled in any battle known to history. What does that prove? Why, that the Commune was not the people's own government but the usurpation of a handful of criminals! The women of Paris joyfully give up their lives at the barricades and on the place of execution. What does this prove? Why, that the demon of the Commune has changed them into Megaeras and Hecates![35] The moderation of the Commune during two months of undisputed sway is equalled only by the heroism of its defence. What does that prove? Why, that for months the Commune carefully hid, under a mask of moderation and humanity, the blood-thirstiness of its fiendish instincts, to be let loose in the hour of its agony!

The working men's Paris, in the act of its heroic self-holocaust, involved in its flames buildings and monuments. While tearing to pieces the living body of the proletariat, its rulers must no longer expect to return triumphantly into the intact architecture of their abodes. The Government of Versailles cries, "Incendiarism!" and whispers this cue to all its agents, down to the remotest hamlet, to hunt up its enemies everywhere as suspect of professional incendiarism. The bourgeoisie of the whole world, which looks complacently upon the wholesale massacre after the battle, is convulsed by horror at the desecration of brick and mortar!

When governments give state-licences to their navies to "kill, *burn* and destroy," is that a licence for incendiarism? When the British troops wantonly set fire to the Capitol at Washington and to the summer palace of the Chinese Emperor, was that incendiarism? When the Prussians, not for military reasons, but out of the mere spite of revenge, burned down, by the help of petroleum, towns like Châteaudun and innumerable villages, was that incendiarism?

When Thiers, during six weeks, bombarded Paris, under the pretext that he wanted to set fire to those houses only in which there were people, was that incendiarism?—In war, fire is an arm as legitimate as any. Buildings held by the enemy are shelled to set them on fire. If their defenders have to retire, they themselves light the flames to prevent the attackers from making use of the buildings. To be burnt down has always been the inevitable fate of all buildings situated in the front of battle of all the regular armies of the world. But in the war of the enslaved against their enslavers, the only justifiable war in history, this is by no means to hold good! The Commune used fire strictly as a means of defence. They used it to stop up to the Versailles troops those long, straight avenues which Haussmann had expressly opened to artillery-fire; they used it to cover their retreat, in the same way as the Versaillese, in their advance, used their shells which destroyed at least as many buildings as the fire of the Commune. It is a matter of dispute, even now, which buildings were set fire to by the defence, and which by the attack. And the defence resorted to fire only then, when the Versaillese troops had already commenced their wholesale murdering of prisoners.—Besides, the Commune had, long before, given full public notice that, if driven to extremities, they would bury themselves under the ruins of Paris, and make Paris a second Moscow, as the Government of Defence, but only as a cloak for its treason, had promised to do. For this purpose Trochu had found them the petroleum. The Commune knew that its opponents cared nothing for the lives of the Paris people, but cared much for their own Paris buildings. And Thiers, on the other hand, had given them notice that he would be implacable in his vengeance. No sooner had he got his army ready on one side, and the Prussians shutting up the trap on the other, than he proclaimed: "I shall be pitiless! The expiation will be complete, and justice will be stern!" If the acts of the Paris working men were vandalism, it was the vandalism of defence in despair, not the vandalism of triumph, like that which the Christians perpetrated upon the really priceless art treasures of heathen antiquity; and even that vandalism has been justified by the historian as an unavoidable and comparatively trifling concomitant to the titanic struggle between a new society arising and an old one breaking down. It was still less the vandalism of Haussmann, razing historic Paris to make place for the Paris of the sightseer!

But the execution by the Commune of the sixty-four hostages, with the Archbishop of Paris at their head! The bourgeoisie and its army in June, 1848, re-established a custom which had long disappeared from the practice of war—the shooting of their defenceless prisoners. This brutal custom has since been more or less strictly adhered to by the suppressors of all popular commotions in Europe and India; thus proving that it constitutes a real "progress of civilization!" On the other hand, the Prussians, in France, had re-established the practice of taking hostages—innocent men, who, with their lives, were to answer to them for the acts of others. When Thiers, as we have seen, from the very beginning of the conflict, enforced the humane practice of shooting down the Communal prisoners, the Commune, to protect their lives, was obliged to resort to the Prussian practice of securing hostages. The lives of the hostages had been forfeited over and over again by the continued shooting of prisoners on the part of the Versaillese. How could they be spared any longer after the carnage with which MacMahon's praetorians [36] celebrated their entrance into Paris? Was even the last check upon the unscrupulous ferocity of bourgeois governments—the taking of hostages—to be made a mere sham of? The real murderer of Archbishop Darboy is Thiers. The Commune again and again had offered to exchange the archbishop, and ever so many priests in the bargain, against the single Blanqui, then in the hands of Thiers. Thiers obstinately refused. He knew that with Blanqui he would give to the Commune a head; while the archbishop would serve his purpose best in the shape of a corpse. Thiers acted upon the precedent of Cavaignac. In June 1848, did not Cavaignac and his men of order raise shouts of horror by stigmatizing the insurgents as the assassins of Archbishop Affre! They knew perfectly well that the archbishop had been shot by the soldiers of order. M. Jacquemet, the archbishop's vicar-general, present on the spot, had immediately afterwards handed them in his evidence to that effect.

All this chorus of calumny, which the Party of Order

never fail, in their orgies of blood, to raise against their victims, only proves that the bourgeois of our days considers himself the legitimate successor to the baron of old, who thought every weapon in his own hand fair against the plebeian, while in the hands of the plebeian a weapon of any kind constituted in itself a crime.

The conspiracy of the ruling class to break down the Revolution by a civil war carried on under the patronage of the foreign invader—a conspiracy which we have traced from the very 4th of September down to the entrance of MacMahon's praetorians through the gate of St. Cloud—culminated in the carnage of Paris. Bismarck gloats over the ruins of Paris, in which he saw perhaps the first instalment of that general destruction of great cities he had prayed for when still a simple Rural in the Prussian *Chambre introuvable* in 1849. He gloats over the cadavers of the Paris proletariat. For him this is not only the extermination of revolution, but the extinction of France, now decapitated in reality, and by the French Government itself. With the shallowness characteristic of all successful statesmen, he sees but the surface of this tremendous historic event. Whenever before has history exhibited the spectacle of a conqueror crowning his victory by turning into, not only the gendarme, but the hired bravo of the conquered Government? There existed no war between Prussia and the Commune of Paris. On the contrary, the Commune had accepted the peace preliminaries, and Prussia had announced her neutrality. Prussia was, therefore, no belligerent. She acted the part of a bravo, a cowardly bravo, because incurring no danger; a hired bravo, because stipulating beforehand the payment of her blood-money of 500 millions on the fall of Paris. And thus, at last, came out the true character of the war, ordained by Providence as a chastisement of godless and debauched France by pious and moral Germany! And this unparalleled breach of the law of nations, even as understood by the old-world lawyers, instead of arousing the "civilized" Governments of Europe to declare the felonious Prussian Government, the mere tool of the St. Petersburg Cabinet, an outlaw amongst nations, only incites them to consider whether the few victims who escape the double cordon around Paris are not to be given up to the hangman at Versailles!

That after the most tremendous war of modern times, the conquering and the conquered hosts should fraternize for the common massacre of the proletariat—this unparalleled event does indicate, not, as Bismarck thinks, the final repression of a new society upheaving, but the crumbling into dust of bourgeois society. The highest heroic effort of which old society is still capable is national war; and this is now proved to be a mere governmental humbug, intended to defer the struggle of classes, and to be thrown aside as soon as that class struggle bursts out into civil war. Class rule is no longer able to disguise itself in a national uniform; the national Governments are *one* as against the proletariat!

After Whit-Sunday, 1871, there can be neither peace nor truce possible between the working men of France and the appropriators of their produce. The iron hand of a mercenary soldiery may keep for a time both classes tied down in common oppression. But the battle must break out again and again in ever-growing dimensions, and there can be no doubt as to who will be the victor in the end,—the appropriating few, or the immense working majority. And the French working class is only the advanced guard of the modern proletariat.

While the European governments thus testify, before Paris, to the international character of class rule, they cry down the International Working Men's Association—the international counter-organization of labour against the cosmopolitan conspiracy of capital—as the fountain head of all these disasters. Thiers denounced it as the despot of labour, pretending to be its liberator. Picard ordered that all communications between the French Internationals and those abroad should be cut off; Count Jaubert, Thiers' mummified accomplice of 1835, declares it the great problem of all civilized governments to weed it out. The Rurals roar against it, and the whole European press joins the chorus. An honourable French writer, completely foreign to our Association, speaks as follows:—"The members of the Central Committee of the National Guard, as well as the greater part of the members of the Commune, are the most active, intelligent, and energetic minds of the International Working Men's Association;... men who are thoroughly honest, sincere, intelligent, devoted, pure, and fanatical in the *good* sense of the word." The police-tinged bourgeois mind naturally figures to itself the International Working Men's Association as acting in the manner of a secret conspiracy, its central body ordering, from time to time, explosions in different countries. Our Association is, in fact, nothing but the international bond between the most advanced working men in the various countries of the civilized world. Wherever, in whatever shape, and under whatever conditions the class struggle obtains any consistency, it is but natural that members of our Association should stand in the foreground. The soil out of which it grows is modern society itself. It cannot be stamped out by any amount of carnage. To stamp it out, the Governments would have to stamp out the despotism of capital over labour—the condition of their own parasitical existence.

Working men's Paris, with its Commune, will be for ever celebrated as the glorious harbinger of a new society. Its martyrs are enshrined in the great heart of the working class. Its exterminators history has already nailed to that eternal pillory from which all the prayers of their priests will not avail to redeem them.

London, *May 30, 1871*

APPENDIXES

I

"The column of prisoners halted in the Avenue Uhrich, and was drawn up, four or five deep, on the footway facing to the road. General Marquis de Galliffet and his staff dismounted and commenced an inspection from the left of the line. Walking down slowly and eyeing the ranks, the General stopped here and there, tapping a man on the shoulder or beckoning him out of the rear ranks. In most cases, without further parley, the individual thus selected was marched out into the centre of the road, where a small supplementary column was, thus, soon formed.... It was evident that there was considerable room for error. A mounted officer pointed out to General Galliffet a man and woman for some particular offence. The woman, rushing out of the ranks, threw herself on her knees, and, with outstretched arms, protested her innocence in passionate terms. The General waited for a pause, and then with most impassible face and unmoved demeanour, said, 'Madame, I have visited every theatre in Paris, your acting will have no effect on me' *('ce n'est pas la peine de jouer la comédie')*.... It was not a good thing on that day to be noticeably taller, dirtier, cleaner, older, or uglier than one's neighbours. One individual in particular struck me as probably owing his speedy release from the ills of this world to his having a broken nose.... Over a hundred being thus chosen, a firing party told off, and the column resumed its march, leaving them behind. A few minutes afterwards a dropping fire in our rear commenced, and continued for over a quarter of an hour. It was the execution of these summarily-convicted wretches." (Paris Correspondent, *Daily News*,[37] June 8th.)

This Galliffet, "the kept man of his wife, so notorious for her shameless exhibitions at the orgies of the Second Empire," went, during the war, by the name of the French "Ensign Pistol."

"The *Temps*[38] which is a careful journal, and not given to sensation, tells a dreadful story of people imperfectly shot and buried before life was extinct. A great number were buried in the square round St. Jacques-la-Bouchière; some of them very superficially. In the daytime the roar of the busy streets prevented any notice being taken; but in the stillness of the night the inhabitants of the houses in the neighbourhood were roused by distant moans, and in the morning a clenched hand was seen protruding through the soil. In consequence of this, exhumations were ordered to take place.... That many wounded have been buried alive I have not the slightest doubt. One case I can vouch for. When Brunel was shot with his mistress on the 24th ult. in the courtyard of a house in the Place Vendôme, the bodies lay there until the afternoon of the 27th. When the burial party came to remove the corpses, they found the woman living still and took her to an ambulance. Though she had received four bullets she is now out of danger." (Paris Correspondent, *Evening Standard*,[39] June 8th.)

II

The following letter appeared in the [London] *Times*[40] of June 13th:

"To the Editor of the *Times*:

"Sir,—On June 6, 1871, M. Jules Favre issued a circular to all the European Powers, calling upon them to hunt down the International Working Men's Association. A few remarks will suffice to characterize that document.

"In the very preamble of our statutes it is stated that the International was founded 'September 28, 1864, at a public meeting held at St. Martin's Hall, Long Acre, London.' For purposes of his own Jules Favre puts back the date of its origin behind 1862.

"In order to explain our principles, he professes to quote 'their (the International's) sheet of the 25th of March, 1869.' And then what does he quote? The sheet of a society which is not the International. This sort of manoeuvre he already recurred to when, still a comparatively young lawyer, he had to defend the *National* newspaper, prosecuted for libel by Cabet. Then he pretended to read extracts from Cabet's pamphlets while reading interpolations of his own —a trick exposed while the Court was sitting, and which, but for the indulgence of Cabet, would have been punished by Jules Favre's expulsion from the Paris bar. Of all the documents quoted by him as documents of the International, not one belongs to the International. He says, for instance, 'The Alliance declares itself Atheist, says the General Council, constituted in London in July 1869.' The General Council never issued such a document. On the contrary, it issued a document which quashed the original statutes of the 'Alliance'—L'Alliance de la Démocratie Socialiste at Geneva—quoted by Jules Favre.

"Throughout his circular, which pretends in part also to be directed against the Empire, Jules Favre repeats against the International but the police inventions of the public prosecutors of the Empire, which broke down miserably even before the law courts of that Empire.

"It is known that in its two addresses (of July and September last) on the late war, the General Council of the International denounced the Prussian plans of conquest against France. Later on, Mr. Reitlinger, Jules Favre's private secretary, applied, though of course in vain, to some members of the General Council for getting up by the Council a demonstration against Bismarck, in favour of the Government of National Defence; they were particularly requested not to mention the republic. The preparations for a demonstration with regard to the expected arrival of Jules Favre in London were made—certainly with the best of intentions—in spite of the General Council, which, in its address of the 9th of September, had distinctly forewarned the Paris workmen against Jules Favre and his colleagues.

"What would Jules Favre say if, in its turn, the International were to send a circular on Jules Favre to all the Cabinets of Europe, drawing their particular attention to the documents published at Paris by the late M. Millière?

"I am, Sir, your obedient servant,

"*John Hales,*

"Secretary to the General Council of the International Working Men's Association.

"London, June 12th, 1871."

In an article on "The International Society and its aims," that pious informer, the London *Spectator* [41] (*June* 24th), amongst other similar tricks, quotes, even more fully than Jules Favre has done, the above document of the "Alliance" as the work of the International, and that eleven days after the refutation had been published in the *Times*. We do not wonder at this Frederick the Great used to say that of all Jesuits the worst are the Protestant ones.

Written by Marx in April-May 1871 and endorsed at a session of the General Council of the International Working Men's Association held on May 30, 1871

Originally published as a separate English pamphlet in London in 1871

German and French editions appeared at the same time

The German text edited by Engels and containing his introduction came out as a separate edition in Berlin in 1891

Printed according to the text of the English pamphlet of 1871

NOTES

[1] *The Anti-Socialist Law* was introduced in Germany in 1878. It provided for the prohibition of all the Social-Democratic organisations, mass labour organisations, the labour press, the confiscation of socialist literature and the persecution of Social-Democrats. The law was repealed in 1890 under the pressure of the mass labour movement. p. 6

[2] At Sedan, on September 2, 1870, the French army was defeated and captured together with the Emperor.
Wilhelmshöhe (near Cassel)—the castle, residence of the Prussian kings. Here the former emperor Napoleon III was held in captivity from September 5, 1870 till March 19, 1871. p. 9

[3] *Possibilists*—exponents of the opportunist trend in the French working-class movement at the end of the 19th century. p. 15

[4] *The plebiscite* was conducted by Napoleon III in May 1870 for the alleged purpose of ascertaining the attitude of the popular masses to the Empire. The questions were so worded that it was impossible to express one's disapproval of his policy without at the same time declaring against all democratic reforms. The sections of the First International in France exposed this demagogic manoeuvre and instructed its members to abstain from voting. p. 19

[5] The Franco-Prussian war began on July 19, 1870. On December 2, 1851, Louis Bonaparte carried out the *coup d'état* which ushered in the Bonapartist system of the Second Empire. p. 20

[6] *Réveil*—Left-republican newspaper founded by Charles Delécluze. It appeared in Paris from 1868 to January 1871. p. 20

[7] *Marseillaise*—Left-republican newspaper published in Paris by Henri Rochefort from December 1869 to September 9, 1870. p. 21

[8] *The Society of December 10* (derived its name from the election of its chief Louis Bonaparte President of the Republic of France on December 10, 1848)—a secret Bonapartist Society set up in 1849, it consisted mainly of declassed elements, political adventurists, representatives of the military, etc. Though the society was officially disbanded on November 1850, its former members continued to

carry on Bonapartist propaganda and took an active part in the *coup d'état* of December 2, 1851. For a detailed characteristic see K. Marx, *The Eighteenth Brumaire of Louis Bonaparte*. p. 21

9 The battle of Sadowa (in Bohemia) was decisive in the Austro-Prussian war of 1866, from which Prussia emerged victorious. p. 21

10 That is, the war against Napoleon I in 1813-15 which resulted in the restoration of the old order and the preservation of the feudal fragmentation of Germany. p. 22

11 On September 4, the Republic was proclaimed in France, and a new government, the so-called "Government of National Defence", was set up. p. 24

12 *The Treaty of Tilsit* was concluded in 1807 between France and Russia after Prussia had been defeated by Napoleon I. p. 27

13 An allusion to the great campaign of meetings, which developed in England among the workers on the initiative of Marx and the General Council of the First International, for securing recognition of the French Republic. p. 31

14 During the Civil War in the USA (1861-65) between the industrial North and the South, where the system of slave plantations prevailed, the English bourgeois press supported the South, that is, slavery. p. 31

15 *Journal Officiel de la République Française*—organ of the Government of the Paris Commune; appeared in Paris from March 19 to May 24, 1871. p. 34

16 *L'Étendard* (The Banner)—the French newspaper with a Bonapartist trend, published in Paris from 1866 to 1868. Its publication was discontinued when it was found that swindles helped finance the newspaper. p. 35

17 The German edition has Karl Vogt; the French, Falstaff.
   Joe Miller—celebrated eighteenth-century English actor. *Karl Vogt*—German bourgeois democrat who became an agent of Napoleon III. *Falstaff*—Shakespearean character portraying the typical rogue and braggart. p. 35

18 In January 1848 Ferdinand II's Neapolitan troops bombarded Palermo in an attempt to crush the popular rebellion which gave the signal for the bourgeois revolution in the Italian states in 1848-49. The cruel bombardment of Messina in the autumn of the same year earned him the nickname of King Bomba. p. 37

19 In April 1849, French troops were sent to Italy to suppress the Italian Revolution. They bombarded revolutionary Rome, in glaring violation of the French Constitution, which provided that the Republic would never employ its forces to suppress the liberty of any people. p. 37

20 *The Party of Order*—the party of the big, conservative bourgeoisie founded in 1848. It was a coalition of the two monarchist factions in France—the Legitimists and Orleanists. From 1849 till the *coup*

d'état of December 2, 1851, it occupied a leading position in the Legislative Assembly of the Second Republic. Louis Bonaparte's clique took advantage of the bankruptcy of the anti-popular policy of the Party of Order to establish the regime of the Second Empire.
p. 38

21 *Legitimists,* supporters of the "legitimate" dynasty of the Bourbons, who were in power in France until 1792, and also during the restoration period (1814-30), and *Orleanists,* supporters of the Orleans dynasty, which had been in power since the revolution of July 1830, and had been overthrown by the 1848 Revolution. p. 40

22 *Chambre introuvable* (Matchless Chamber)—the chamber of deputies in 1815-16 (the first years of the Restoration), which consisted of extreme reactionaries. p. 40

23 *Pourceaugnac*—a character in one of Molière's comedies, typifying the dull-witted, narrow-minded petty landed gentry. p. 40

24 *Assembly of Rurals*—the National Assembly, which opened in Bordeaux on February 12, 1871, had a vast majority of royalists (450 out of 750 deputies)—representatives of the landlords and reactionary elements of town and country. Hence its name of "Assembly of Rurals" or Landlord Chamber. p. 40

25 *Cayenne*—capital of French Guiana in South America; penal settlement and place of exile. p. 43

26 *Le National*—newspaper which appeared in Paris in 1830-51; organ of the bourgeois-republican party. p. 45

27 See Voltaire. *Candide,* Chapter 22. p. 49

28 *Investiture*—in the Middle Ages the act of investing the vassal with the land by the suzerain or installation into an ecclesiastic office. The system of investiture was marked by a complete dependence of those in the lower rungs of the hierarchic ladder on the temporal and spiritual lords. p. 55

29 *Kladderadatsch*—German satirical magazine, that appeared in Berlin from 1848 onwards. *Punch,* weekly, has appeared in London since 1841. p. 56

30 *Vendôme column* was erected in 1806-10 in Place Vendôme in Paris to commemorate the victories of Napoleonic France. On May 16, 1871, the column was pulled down by a decision of the Paris Commune. p. 62

31 *Absentees*—big landlords who never visit their estates. p. 64

32 *Coblenz*—a city in Germany, was the centre of the French counter-revolutionary *émigré* nobles at the time of the French bourgeois revolution of the end of the 18th century. p. 66

33 *Chouans* was the name which the Paris Communards gave to the reactionary detachment of the Versailles army recruited in Brittany by analogy with those who took part in the counter-revolutionary revolt in North-Western France during the French bourgeois revolution at the end of the 18th century. p. 66

³⁴ *Zouaves*—French light infantry (from the name of an Algerian tribe). The first Zouave units were formed in the first third of the 19th century from local Algerian population. Subsequently they were recruited from the French, but the old Oriental uniform was retained. p. 66

³⁵ *Megaera and Hecata*—in ancient Greek mythology goddesses of evil and magic arts. p. 73

³⁶ *Praetorians*—the name given in ancient Rome to the bodyguard of a general or emperor, who kept them. They enjoyed various privileges. Here "praetorians" means the Versailles army. p. 75

³⁷ *Daily News*—English Liberal newspaper, mouthpiece of industrial bourgeoisie, appeared under this title in London from 1846 to 1930. p. 80

³⁸ *Le Temps*—French influential Liberal daily, published in Paris from 1861 to 1943. p. 80

³⁹ *The Evening Standard*—daily English Conservative newspaper published in London from 1857 to 1905. p. 80

⁴⁰ *The Times*—English influential newspaper, founded in 1788, in the seventies of the 19th century it adhered to a Liberal trend. p. 80

⁴¹ *Spectator*—a Liberal weekly, published in London since 1828. p. 82

NAME INDEX

A

Affre (1793-1848): Archbishop of Paris; killed by bullets of government troops while attempting to persuade the insurgent workers, during the uprising of June 1848, to lay down their arms—75

Alexander II (1818-1881): Russian Emperor (1855-1881)—28

Alexandra (1844-1925): daughter of King Christian IX of Denmark; in 1863 married the then Prince of Wales, who in 1901 became the British King Edward VII—46

Aurelle de Paladines, Louis (1804-1877): French general, monarchist, in March 1871 commanded the National Guard of Paris; Deputy to the National Assembly in 1871—41, 42, 44

B

Berry, Duchess de (1798-1870): mother of Count Chambord, Legitimist pretender to French throne. In 1832, tried to raise a revolt in the Vendee aimed at overthrowing Louis Philippe—36

Beslay, Charles (1795-1878): French employer, man of letters and politician, member of the First Internationl, Proudhonist, member of the Paris Commune—39

Bismarck, Otto (1815-1898): statesman and diplomat of Prussia and Germany, Chancellor of German Empire from 1871 to 1890—9, 21, 28, 34, 35, 38, 40, 42, 56, 63, 69, 76, 81

Blanqui, Louis-Auguste (1805-1881): French revolutionist, utopian Communist, organised some secret societies and conspiracies; took an active part in the revolutions of 1830 and 1848; leader of the proletarian movement in France; one of the leaders of the uprising of October 31, 1870 in Paris; was repeatedly thrown into prison—12, 41, 45, 75

Bonaparte: See Napoleon I

Bonaparte, Louis: See Napoleon III

Brunel, Antoine-Magloire (b. 1830): French officer, Blanquist, member of Paris Commune, member of Central Committee of National Guard, in May 1871 he was heavily wounded by the Versaillese—80

C

Cabet, Etienne (1788-1856): French utopian Communist,

author of **Travels in Icaria**—81

Calonne, Charles-Alexandre (1734-1802): Finance Minister of Louis XVI (1783-1787)—66

Cavaignac, Louis-Eugène (1802-1857): French general. Received dictatorial powers from Constituent Assembly, and put down June uprising (1848) of Paris proletariat with the utmost cruelty—75

Changarnier, Nicolas-Anne-Théodule (1793-1877): French general, monarchist; took part in quelling June uprising in Paris (1848)—47

Coetlogon, Louis-Charles (1814-1886): French official, Prefect—46

Corbon, Claude Anthime (1808-1891): French politician; member of Constituent Assembly (1848-1849); after September 4, 1870, Mayor of a Paris arrondissement; member of National Assembly (1871)—33

Cousin-Montauban, Charles Guillaume, Comte de Palikao (1796-1878): French general, Bonapartist, in August-September 1870 was War Minister and Prime Minister—41

D

Darboy, Georges (1813-1871): Archbishop of Paris, executed as hostage by Communards—75

Desmarêt: French gendarmerie officer, participated in atrocities against Communards—48

Douay, Felix (1816-1879): French general; taken prisoner together with Napoleon III at Sedan in Franco-Prussian War; one of butchers of Paris Commune—71

Dufaure, Armand-Jules (1798-1881): French lawyer, minister under Louis Philippe and Second Republic, Minister of Justice in Thiers government—41, 47, 67, 68

Duval, Emile Victor (1841-1871): French worker, member of First International, general of Paris Commune; shot by Versaillists during sortie on April 3-4, 1871—48

E

Espartero, Baldomero (1793-1879): Spanish general, leader of Progressive Party, Regent of Spain (1841-1843) and Premier (1854-1856)—37

Eudes, Emile (1843-1888): Blanquist, member of Paris Commune; until April 4 was military delegate of Commune—12

F

Favre, Jules (1809-1880): French politician, bourgeois republican, member of Government of National Defence (1870); took part in suppression of Paris Commune—33-35, 39, 42, 45, 63, 70, 80-82

Ferdinand II (1810-1859): King of Naples; was given sobriquet "King Bomba" for bombarding Palermo and Messina during 1848 Revolution—36

Ferry, Jules (1832-1893): French lawyer and politician; one of hangmen of Paris Commune; Premier (1880-1881 and 1883-1885)—35

Flourens, Gustave (1838-1871): French Blanquist revolutionist, member of Military Commission of Paris Commune; brutally murdered by Versaillese during sortie of Commune troops on April 3, 1871—41, 45, 48

Frederick II (1712-1786): King of Prussia (1740-1786)—82

G

Galliffet, Gaston (1830-1909): French general, one who butchered Paris Commune—48, 49, 79, 80

Gambetta, Léon (1838-1882): French statesman; bourgeois republican; member of Government of National Defence (1870-1871); Prime Minister and Minister of Foreign Affairs (1881-1882)—34

Ganesco, Grégory (ab. 1830-1877): French journalist, native of Rumania, during Second Empire was Bonapartist, then supporter of Thiers government—61

Gorchakov, Alexander Mikhailovich (1798-1883): Russian diplomat and statesman, Foreign Minister (1856-1882)—28

Guiod, Alphonse Simon (b. 1805): French general, took part in Franco-Prussian War; Artillery Commander-in-Chief during siege of Paris, 1870-1871—34

Guizot, François-Pierre (1787-1874): French bourgeois historian and statesman; monarchist—37

H

Hales, John: member of General Council, First International (1869-1872)—82

Haussmann, Georges-Eugène (1809-1891): Prefect of Paris under Second Empire; reconstructed the capital in the interests of bourgeoisie—62, 74, 75

Heeckeren (d'Anthès), Georges-Charles (1812-1895): French nobleman, lived a long period in Russia, murderer of Alexander Pushkin; became Bonapartist; one of active participants in *coup d'état* of December 2, 1851—46

Hervé, Edouard (1835-1899): French monarchist publicist—72

Hohenzollerns: dynasty of Electors of Brandenburg (1415-1701), Kings of Prussia (1701-1918) and German Emperors (1871-1918)—21

Huxley, Thomas Henry (1825-1895): English natural scientist, friend and disciple of Darwin—58

J

Jacquemet: French priest, in 1848 was Vicar-General of Archbishop of Paris—75

Jaubert, François (1798-1874): French politician, monarchist, Minister of Public Works in Thiers Cabinet (1840), member of National Assembly, 1871—77

K

King Bomba—See Ferdinand II

L

Laffitte, Jacques (1767-1844): French banker—36

Lecomte, Claude-Martin (1817-1871): French general, took part in nocturnal raid on Montmartre on March 18, 1871; killed by his own men who went over to the side of the people—45, 46, 50, 68, 69, 70

Le Flô, Adolphe-Emmanuel-Charles (1804-1887): French

general, monarchist, member of Constituent and Legislative assemblies (1848-1851), War Minister (1870-1871)—46, 49

Louis Bonaparte—See Napoleon III

Louis Napoleon—See Napoleon III

Louis XVI (1754-1793): King of France (1774-1792)—11

Louis Philippe (1773-1850): King of France (1830-1848)—8, 36, 38, 39, 45, 56, 68

M

MacMahon, Marie-Edme-Patrice Maurice (1808-1893): French marshal; in 1871 commanded Versailles troops; one of butchers of Commune; President of Third Republic (1873-1879)—71, 76

Markovsky—tsarist government agent in France; in 1871 was one of Thiers' men—61

Marx, Karl (1818-1883)—5, 6, 15

Millière, Jean-Baptiste (1817-1871): Left Proudhonist, journalist, participated in Paris Commune; shot by Versaillists in May, 1871—34, 82

Montesquieu, Charles (1689-1755): French historian and writer, ideologist of constitutional monarchy—55

N

Napoleon I (1769-1821)—11, 16, 23, 24, 38, 61

Napoleon III (Louis Bonaparte) (1808-1873)—5, 8, 19, 21, 24, 28-31, 32, 34, 38, 39, 40, 43, 44, 45, 51, 56, 60-62, 65, 68, 69

O

Orleans, Duke of—See Louis Philippe

Orleans: French royal dynasty—62

P

Palikao—See Cousin-Montauban

Pène, Henri (1830-1888): French journalist, monarchist, Legitimist, then Bonapartist; one of organizers of counter-revolutionary action in Paris, March 22, 1871—47

Pic, Jules: French journalist, Bonapartist, responsible publisher of *Etendard* newspaper—35

Picard, Arthur (b. 1825): French politician and journalist, monarchist, member of Chamber of Deputies from 1876—35

Picard, Ernest (1821-1877): Finance Minister in Government of National Defence, Minister of Interior in Thiers government—35, 42, 48, 77

Pietri (1820-1902): active participant in *coup d'état* of December 2, 1851, Prefect of police during Second Empire—21, 66

Pouyer-Quertier, August-Thomas (1820-1891): Bonapartist, Finance Minister in Thiers government (1871-1872)—42, 69

Proudhon, Pierre-Joseph (1809-1865)—14, 15

S

Saisset, Jean (1810-1879): French Vice-Admiral, monarchist—47

Simon, Jules (1814-1896): French publicist, Minister of Public Education in Government of National Defence—42

Sulla, Lucius Cornelius (138-78 B. C.): Roman dictator—39, 71

Susanne, Louis (1810-1876): French general, War Minister from February 1871—34

T

Tacitus, Publius Cornelius (c. 55-120 A. D.): Roman historian—72

Taillefer: participant in shady affair connected with publication of Bonapartist paper *Etendard*—35

Tamerlane (Timur) (1336-1405): Central Asian captain and conqueror—48

Tamisier, François Laurent Alphonse (1809-1880): French general, republican, Commander-in-Chief of Paris National Guard—45

Thiers, Louis-Adolphe (1797-1877): French bourgeois historian and statesman, hangman of Paris Commune—10, 12, 20, 32-33, 36-43, 46-50, 52, 53, 59, 61-63, 65-71, 74-75, 77

Thomas, Clément (1809-1871): head of Paris National Guard; killed during Paris Commune by troops that went over to the side of the people—45-46, 50, 68, 69, 70

Tolain, Henri-Louis (1828-1897): French worker, one of founders of French section of First International, Proudhonist; during Paris Commune crossed over to Versaillists, and was expelled from International—49

Trochu, Louis-Jules (1815-1896): French general, head of Government of National Defence (1870), one of hangmen of Paris Commune—32-34, 39, 43, 45, 46, 74

V

Vaillant, Eduard (1840-1915): Blanquist, member of General Council of First International and of Paris Commune; one of founders of French Socialist Party, subsequently a reformist—14

Valentin, Louis Ernest: French general, Bonapartist, Acting Chief of Police of Paris on eve of uprising of March 18, 1871—41-42, 66

Vinoy, Joseph (1800-1880): French general, Bonapartist, commanded Versailles army during Paris Commune, one of hangmen of Paris Commune—41-42, 44, 46, 48

Voltaire, François Marie (Arouet) (1694-1778)—49

W

Wales, Princess of: See Alexandra

William I (1797-1888)—24, 70

REQUEST TO READERS

Progress Publishers would be glad to have your opinion of this book, its translation and design and any suggestions you may have for future publications.

Please send all your comments to 17, Zubovsky Boulevard, Moscow, USSR